Also by Susan Walberg

AVAILABLE ON AMAZON

The Insider's Guide to Compliance

The Insider's Guide to Compliance for Physician Practices

The Hippocratic Deception (a novel)

Finding Maslow (a novel)

Angels of Deception (a novel)—coming soon!

HEALTHCARE TECHNOLOGY
LAW AND COMPLIANCE

The User-Friendly Guide to
Healthtech Law

SUSAN LEE WALBERG, JD MPA CHC

ISBN: 978-0-999-8605-5-7 Trade Paperback
ISBN: 978-0-999-8605-6-4 eBook

Healthcare Texchnology, Law and Compliance
The User Friendly Guide to Healthtech Law
by Susan Lee Walberg JD MPA CHC

Cover design by Glen M. Edelstein, Hudson Valley Book Design
Printed in the United States of America

CONTENTS

INTRODUCTION

The purpose of this book is to help healthcare technology start-ups, investors, healthcare providers, and any other healthcare-related organization understand the applicable laws and regulations for developing and using technology in healthcare. Healthcare consumers, too, may find this book useful in understanding how, for instance, their health data is being secured and what privacy rights they have when using the various types of healthcare technology.

Since the onset of the COVID pandemic, the practice of healthcare has dramatically changed, with telemedicine, which relies on technology, becoming a significant part of many healthcare practices. The use of technology for scheduling, managing patient care, remote monitoring, telehealth visits, and a plethora of other healthcare activities has exploded. Mobile healthcare services, usually managed or coordinated through technology solutions, have also seen significant growth. Healthcare devices are another growing market as innovation and advances in technology create more ways to monitor and even manage patient health. And artificial intelligence, or AI, with its potential to reduce errors and save clinicians' time, is the hot topic discussed at the top of many healthcare publications and podcasts.

One of the challenges in these rapidly changing circumstances is that the existing laws and regulations were written for a different world, not this current one. A prominent example is the regulation of healthcare devices. With the advent of apps that can actually perform the same function as desktop tools that track and measure a patient's vitals, the Food and Drug

Administration has designated some mobile apps as "medical devices" so that it can monitor them for safety.

Another big change is the proliferation of healthcare apps. Patients are now managing their healthcare from their smartphones, which raises a variety of issues, from privacy and security to patient safety. Patient data is being collected and transmitted remotely, and the artificial intelligence tools in the apps collate, interpret, and make recommendations to clinicians based on programmed algorithms. Add to that the growth in telehealth services and we are looking at a whole new realm that the current regulatory framework is struggling to handle.

The COVID pandemic added impetus to the spread of healthcare-technology-related tools and services, but this movement was already well underway as a shift in demographics (aging population) and reimbursement models moved away from fee-for-service toward a more outcome-based approach (value-based care). Now that we are living in a post-COVID world, healthcare no longer looks the same. It's improbable we will ever return to the previous model.

The Health Insurance Portability and Accountability Act of 1996 (otherwise known as HIPAA) was written in a different world, too. It is not surprising that confusion reigns when a provider, device manufacturer, or app developer tries to comply with existing regulations. Which laws apply, and to whom? What do they require? And how can organizations navigate this confusing morass? Is it only HIPAA that a tech developer needs to worry about, or is there more to this whole "compliance" thing?

Understanding the regulatory framework is not just the right thing to do—it's a business necessity. For providers, developers, regulators, and, yes, patients to embrace this new world of healthcare, they need to trust the safety, efficacy, and cybersecurity of the various tools. Before investors open their checkbooks, they will want assurances, as well, that the health technology being developed will not only do what it claims to do but also help providers and patients achieve better outcomes, lowered costs, or increased efficiency without creating risks to patients.

There are many stakeholders in healthcare technology: everyone from device manufacturers around the globe and small start-ups with the next great idea for a revolutionary healthcare app to the patients, providers, investors, health plans, and regulators who will welcome this health tech into the new world of healthcare. Clinicians are seeing opportunities to streamline care and create new collaborations, often using technology as part of that model. Patients, providers, and healthcare plans rely on technology daily and must trust that it will not create risk before they can fully embrace new tools with the potential to improve life for everyone. Investors who are funding this new world of healthcare also must have confidence that they are backing a product or service that will truly improve patients' lives and meet the identified financial goals. The trick is fitting the new technologies, as well as new models of care, such as value-based care, into the existing (but also evolving) regulatory framework while still focusing on patient care and financial efficiency.

Although I can't realistically address every type of technology used in every type of care situation (they will undoubtedly change before this book goes to print!), I can provide enough context so that you can make a solid application of the regulatory requirements to the various types of healthcare technologies you work with. At a minimum, you will know where to look to find the current state of regulations and enforcement mechanisms. I've also included relevant case studies about compliance breakdowns and alerts from government agencies to illuminate how compliance, or lack thereof, can play out in the real world.

Different laws apply and a range of regulatory agencies have been given, or have assumed, oversight of the various healthcare technology applications we are discussing. So, with that idea in mind, starting in Chapter 2, I begin each chapter by identifying "who needs to read this." Some information might apply only to a healthcare provider, for instance, as opposed to a small tech start-up. I've tried to make the stakeholders clear throughout because we really are dealing with a patchwork of laws and oversight at this point. I also have embedded to-do's, because learning which laws apply is important, but knowing what to do with that knowledge is even better.

One disclaimer: Laws and regulations, and even enforcement, have been changing quickly because of the growth in this arena, so please stay on top of changes in the applicable laws. This book is not intended as legal advice but rather as a snapshot of how you could apply current laws to various types of healthcare technology in the current market. I encourage everyone to monitor the laws and regulatory agencies referenced herein to stay on top of this shifting landscape.

With that being said, let's get started.

PART I

An Overview of Healthcare Technology

CHAPTER 1

Healthcare Technology: What Is It?

Depending on who you are, specific images might come to mind when you hear the terms *healthcare technology, health tech,* and *telehealth.* Given the rate of change and growth in this area, these terms can be challenging to define in a universally agreed manner. Similarly, with the rapid advances in health technology being made every day, it's impossible for one book to cover every facet and remain current.

For our purposes, I primarily focus on describing the laws, regulations, and enforcement activities that apply to healthcare apps and connected devices that contain or transmit Protected Health Information (PHI). I provide an overview of how virtual care and telehealth providers can remain in compliance with the health tech they use as well as other legal requirements that apply to telehealth practices.

After the changes made during the COVID pandemic, the world of virtual care and telehealth exploded into a whole new type of care. Often, users do not understand how the laws apply to the two types of technology (*apps* and *devices*) and may miss important exposures during security risk assessments. (I discuss the HIPAA Security Rule in depth in Chapter 2.) Health tech compliance is a lot to keep up with, and this doesn't even include compliance for the latest boom to affect healthcare: artificial intelligence (AI). (Don't worry, we'll be discussing AI as well.)

Keep in mind that one practice or even one patient's care plan may employ various types of health technology, so the range of laws and regulatory requirements that apply will vary accordingly. With each type of technology,

I provide a summary of which laws likely apply and which agencies you can look to for guidance and oversight. If there are recommended actions to maintain compliance, I include those too.

The best place to start in a complex topic is by defining terms. I try to use terms that best describe the technology we are discussing because the terminology offered by Health and Human Services (HHS), below, is very broad and somewhat generic. Here, I list the general categories as outlined by HHS, but you will see throughout the book that these "buckets" can include a variety of technologies and, as a result, a range of regulatory requirements apply. This is just a high-level schematic for organizing the concepts/activities to start. We'll get more granular later.

Mobile health (mHealth). The use of a digital device such as a smartphone or something worn by the patient, commonly called a "wearable," that is used to support patient health. Examples include:

- Fitness trackers
- Phone applications that record a patient's exercise
- Automatic reminders such as when to take medicine
- Storage devices for information or educational materials such as discharge instructions

Remote patient monitoring (RPM). The transmission of patient data and clinical information to the provider either through in-home devices or information entered and transmitted electronically by the patient. Examples of remote patient monitoring devices include:

- Blood pressure monitors
- Pacemakers
- Glucose meters
- Oximeters
- Wireless scales
- Heart rate monitors[1]

Synchronous care. This is what people generally think of as "telehealth," such as a video appointment with a provider or a phone check-in. Synchronous care takes place directly between patient and provider with a real-time interaction.

Asynchronous care. As you might expect, asynchronous care is the opposite of synchronous care—it is "store and forward" patient care. In this model, patient information is collected and stored, usually in the cloud, for the provider to review later. Examples include patients filling out intake forms and health history/surveys online, and secured messaging between provider and patient.

Although these buckets may be useful to HHS, they are really overly broad for our purposes because one type of device or activity could have a range of regulatory requirements depending on the specific details of that device or whether the activity involves multiple technologies. For instance, remote patient monitoring can be achieved, in part, through the use of a health app on a smartphone. A smartphone may be considered a "wearable" by HHS, but it also can be used to take pictures or to text patient information, so it comes under Health Insurance Portability and Accountability Act of 1996 (HIPAA) regulations because it transmits health information. In that context, it is more often referred to as a "mobile device." The terminology can be confusing, in part, I believe, because this has all evolved so rapidly and continues to change.

Now let's move from the general to the more specific. For each type of tool or device, I'll identify which agencies have been engaged in rulemaking, enforcement, and/or oversight. The chapters that follow will give you more details on the specific laws and additional examples of enforcement.

Healthcare Applications ("Apps")

An *app* is a small program that can be loaded onto a phone or mobile device to perform a specialized function. In healthcare, various privacy and security rules and other regulations govern the different types of healthcare apps. Designation of the types of healthcare apps that follows is my own, and I use these categories just to clarify and simplify discussion of the applicable regulations.

Medical Apps

Medical apps are applications healthcare providers and insurance companies and other similar organizations use. These apps may be used to store patients' lab or radiology results or they may be used to coordinate patient care. They might be a tool for conducting telehealth visits, sending notifications or patient updates to providers, or identifying treatment options.

Medical apps that are sponsored or used by a provider or health plan are typically covered under HIPAA, either as a *Covered Entity* or a *Business Associate*. (See Chapter 2 for definitions of HIPAA-related terms.) Note that I am not referring here to apps that function as medical devices, which are described below. Also, just to be clear, not every app a physician practice recommends would be an app that is covered by HIPAA. But if it is one used by a practice in conjunction with patient care, then HIPAA does apply.

Personal Apps

Personal healthcare apps are those that an individual can get at an app store to track and manage their diet, exercise, or specific health conditions. There are apps for mental health, diabetes, and, of course, COVID, to name just a few. Many of these apps are free. Consumers enter and track their personal health data through the use of these apps. The problem, in terms of privacy and security, is that these apps provide little to no protection of that personal information, and users' personal health data has often been sold or shared with a variety of players, such as Google and Facebook, and others. The many thousands of apps that are selected and used by consumers to manage illnesses, track fitness, and provide other health-related services do not usually fall under HIPAA's requirements and have been, for the most part, unregulated.

Historically, the Federal Trade Commission (FTC), the agency responsible for consumer protection, hasn't really been on the radar in terms of regulatory oversight in this arena, but this is changing. FTC now includes *cybersecurity failure* as an "unfair trade practice," thereby fitting personal apps into FTC's purview under the Federal Trade Commission Act (FTCA). In a number of cases, some included in this book, the FTCA has been increasingly used in this manner.

The FTC is not relying solely on the FTCA to pursue bad actors in the healthcare app space, however. The FTC's Breach Notification Rule has been in effect since 2009, but was pretty quiet in terms of enforcement. All of this changed with a September 15, 2021, policy statement in which FTC clarified the scope of the existing Breach Notification Rule.[2] And on May 18, 2023, FTC came out with proposed changes to the Health Breach Notification Rule (HBNR), explaining its applicability to apps and other connected devices.[3] The proposed changes largely reflect the clarifications issued in the 2021 policy statement and were finalized on April 26, 2024. Continue watching the FTC for ongoing guidance and enforcement activity, particularly if you are in the health tech space but not covered under HIPAA.

Regulatory Oversight of Apps: FTC. HHS could have oversight if a personal app is developed or used by a HIPAA Covered Entity and is provided to patients for using with their Protected Health Information (PHI).

Case in Point: Flo

Flo, a fertility-related app, made the news in 2021 when it was discovered that the app was sharing user data with third-party app analytic and marketing services such as Facebook and Google. Findings include violating a stated commitment to privacy by sharing in-app activities such as users' period data and fertility information with Facebook and Google without the users being able to block such distribution.

Flo, with over a hundred million users, has reached a settlement agreement with the FTC that includes a requirement for its privacy practices to be reviewed and (presumably) overhauled and allowing patients to consent to their data usage. According to the FTC:

> As part of the settlement, Flo Health must notify affected users about the disclosure of their health information and instruct any third party that received users' health information to destroy that data. Flo also is prohibited from misrepresenting

---

- the purposes for which it (or entities to whom it discloses data) collects, maintains, uses, or discloses the data;
- how much consumers can control these data uses;
- its compliance with any privacy, security, or compliance program; and
- how it collects, maintains, uses, discloses, deletes, or protects users' personal information.

Flo compounded its problems when it did not stop its data-sharing practice until news of the pending settlement was made public; at that point, hundreds of complaints were received and the company stopped its data-sharing practices.

This case was the first in which the FTC issued a Notice requirement for sharing consumers' private health information without consent. One interesting point, which was documented by two FTC commissioners, was the failure to employ the Breach Notification Rule in this case, which instead relied on the Federal Trade Commission Act (FTCA).[4] More recent cases have corrected this approach, but the FTC has also continued to use the FTCA for its "deceptive or unfair trade practices" provisions.[5]

Medical Device Apps

There is one type of application that the Food and Drug Administration (FDA) considers a medical device: apps that are intended to be used "for the diagnosis of disease or other conditions, or the cure, mitigation, treatment, or prevention of disease, or intended to affect the structure or any function of the body of man" under Section 201(h) of the Food, Drug, and Cosmetic Act (FDCA).

In general, if the purpose or function of an app is to assist in performing a medical device function, the app is treated as a medical device under the FDA. For instance, if an app on a smartphone or other handheld device analyzes and interprets electrocardiogram (EKG) waveforms while monitoring the patient's cardiac irregularities, it is considered analogous to those software programs used in a practice that perform the same function and that are regulated as medical devices.

The intent of the FDA is to ensure patient safety with the use of devices that could compromise or risk patient health. This oversight is limited to devices marketed and offered to perform medical device functions. Chapter 4 discusses Software as a Medical Device (SaMD), which is also subject to medical device regulations.

Regulatory Oversight of Apps: FDA. (Chapter 4 provides more information on FDA regulations and enforcement activities related to medical device apps.) HHS also has oversight if the app was developed by or for a Covered Entity and serves to collect, store, or transmit patient information on behalf of that Covered Entity.

Connected Devices and Wearables

The use of medical devices that collect and transmit health information is, as with apps, increasing dramatically. Devices that actually monitor a patient's health and then send that data to the physician or hospital may be connected to home networks, public Wi-Fi, or cellular networks, thereby increasing the variety of ways this data can be hacked or otherwise compromised.

There are several types of connected devices, including the following.

Stationary Medical Devices

These include ultrasound, MRI, and CT machines that send images or results to the patient's electronic medical record. Although the devices themselves are not high risk for security breaches (nobody is generally walking off with a CT scanner), the transmission of results opens them up to potential hacking or other security failures.

I mention stationary medical devices primarily as a reminder that sources of electronic PHI (ePHI) must be evaluated as part of a risk analysis, as discussed in Chapter 2 on HIPAA.

Implantable Medical Devices

Implantable medical devices, or IMDs, include devices such as pacemakers that are inserted into a patient and that send data to the provider. These devices not only monitor but also interact with the patient's body.

Information from the device may be available to both the patient and the provider, allowing for real-time adjustments. Though the technology of these devices is incredible, so too is the risk, however remote, if one of these devices were hacked or otherwise tampered with.

Implantable devices can be controlled wirelessly (i.e., by Bluetooth, connected through a patient's smartphone) or via the internet, which opens up the possibility of hackers anywhere in the world potentially gaining access. It doesn't take a huge amount of imagination to realize the risks here. Imagine, for instance, a political figure with a pacemaker. One sophisticated hacker could potentially cause life-threatening changes to an implanted device.

The security of these devices can be compromised in several ways. First, the actual communications of a wireless IMD can be accessed if there is no encryption or authentication protocols in place, thus exposing sensitive information. Even if a device's communications are protected by encryption—which is not the case for many existing devices—the mere presence and patterns of such signals can provide information that could be valuable for an attacker.[6]

The next type of risk is through access to the actual base station or programmer itself. Communications with remote devices, whether wirelessly or over the internet, can be compromised by the introduction of malicious code. This can be particularly dangerous considering the increasing use of IMDs in conjunction with smartphones and tablets. Malware inserted into the programmer could alter the function of the IMD.

In addition to the technical security risks, the general human-factor risks I discuss throughout this book are also in play. Common issues such as failure to sign off a workstation and poor password control can also open up risks for IMDs. Although these risks can be monitored and mitigated to some extent in a practice setting, there are also risk factors on the other end, in the patient's home or a cybercafe, and with their general security measures, or lack thereof, for their phone or tablet used to interact with the IMD.

Case in Point: Medtronic

Medtronic is a medical device company. In 2019, researchers discovered that the means Medtronic used to connect to implanted devices had no encryption, leaving it open to potential hackers. The mechanism used by

Medtronic, Conexus Radio Frequency Telemetry Protocol, also had no means of authentication in addition to other vulnerabilities that left it exposed to attackers within radio range. What this means, in practical terms, is that a hacker could intercept the communications and modify the functionality, in addition to accessing sensitive data.

The US Department of Homeland Security's Cybersecurity and Infra-structure Security Agency (CISA), which rated the severity of Medtronic's risk at 9.3 out of a possible 10 points, issued an advisory stating that only a low level of skill was necessary to exploit the product. When the researchers conducted testing, they were able to make unauthorized changes and actu-ally change the shocks the device delivered to the patient. The researchers were also able to read and rewrite the firmware used to operate the implant.

Although this is certainly alarming, it is important to note that a series of specific events would need to occur and the hacker would need to have very specific knowledge to actually cause harm. Also, this was in 2019, and Medtronic has been working on its security since that time.[7]

When your practice is considering purchasing any implantable device, include your security expert in product demo sessions so they can ask critical questions, such as these:

- Are the device's data storage and communications encrypted?
- How is private data protected?
- How is access authenticated? What are the access controls?
- How is inappropriate access detected?
- How is data retention managed?

Wearable Medical Devices ("Wearables") and Remote Patient Monitoring (RPM)

Cardioverter defibrillators and patches are examples of wearable devices that monitor patient activity without being inserted into the patient's body. Smart watches and wearable activity trackers also track and report patient status.

Wearables can operate totally anonymously when they do not collect any identifying information from the user, or they can be customized and use personal health data. The risks and requirements vary depending on the type of device, unsurprisingly. Devices that collect and transmit personal health information are governed by HIPAA, whereas a simple pedometer is not.

It is important to keep in mind that even anonymous devices can present privacy concerns because of their very nature: if a wearable device flashes the user's health information on their wrist, for instance, it's obvious whose information is being displayed. If it transmits that data to the patient's healthcare provider, it's now in HIPAA territory.

When evaluating wearable medical devices and remote patient monitoring (RPM) for compliance issues, consider not only HIPAA but also the FDA to determine whether your device is classified as a medical device. In the event of data breaches or inappropriate sharing of health data, the FTC may play a role, but typically devices that transmit patient data come under HIPAA because they are being used by a HIPAA Covered Entity. Just be aware that the FTC can step in, though, if a developer misrepresents the device's privacy and security safeguards.

Digital therapeutics are therapeutic interventions driven by specific software programs that aim to prevent and/or treat various medical conditions. Digital therapeutics, wearables, and even AI work together to help improve timeliness and quality of care, which are particularly important for distant or disabled patients, who benefit from remote monitoring. Because these therapeutics provide direct care and intervention for patients, they are covered by the FDA and require approvals, just like medical devices.

Regulatory Oversight for Medical Devices: Health and Human Services; HIPAA; the FDA if it's a medical device; and potentially FTC if the issue is not addressed by HIPAA and is a cybersecurity or unfair business practice issue.

Case in Point: Fitness Trackers

Here is an excerpt from a recent news article detailing the data breach of a popular wearable medical device:

In September 2021, over 61 million fitness tracker records from both Apple and Fitbit were exposed online in a wearable device data breach, according to a report from WebsitePlanet and independent

---

cybersecurity researcher Jeremiah Fowler.

Researchers found that the data breach stemmed from GetHealth, a New York–based health and wellness company that allows users to unify their wearable device, medical device, and app data. The exposed data belonged to wearable device users around the world and contained names, birthdates, weight, height, gender, and geographical location.

The database was not password-protected, and the information was clearly identifiable in plain text. Fitbit was listed in over 2,700 records, and Apple's Healthkit was mentioned over 17,000 times.

Researchers also discovered that the files showed where the data was stored, along with a blueprint of the network's backend operations, making it an extremely easy target for cyberattacks.

Fowler said he immediately sent a responsible disclosure notice of his findings and received a reply from GetHealth the next day. The company confirmed that the data had since been secured.

"Fitness trackers by their design are intended to understand and improve our health by providing critical information that could indicate health risks," the report pointed out.

"In the process of collecting this information on users the device must be able to access very private information about our lives, health, and much more."

Bad actors can use this highly personal data to send personalized phishing emails, commit fraud, and obtain even more personal information.

"We are not implying any wrongdoing by GetHealth, their customers, or partners," the report continued.

"Nor are we implying that any customer or user data was at risk. We were unable to determine the exact number of affected individuals before the database was restricted from public access. We are only highlighting our discovery to raise awareness of the dangers and cyber security vulnerabilities posed by IoT [Internet of Things], wearable devices, fitness and health trackers, and how that data is stored."

That convenience comes with a cost for users, and a responsibility

> to protect private data for companies. At this time, there are no univer-sal privacy standards for wearable devices, which gives companies the ability to use the data for advertising or third-party sharing. . . .
>
> However, the US Food and Drug Administration (FDA) classi-fied Fitbit as a Class II medical device in 2020 and later gave FDA clearance for its electrocardiogram function.[8]

Mobile Devices

A discussion of healthcare technology risks would not be complete without covering mobile devices. Although the Centers for Medicare & Medicaid Services (CMS) includes these in the mHealth category, I see the use of mobile devices as being much broader. Although mobile devices such as smartphones and tablets have presented risks and challenges in healthcare for a number of years, the massive increases in the volume of remote workers, the use of health apps by providers and consumers, and the market for mobile healthcare services have all raised the demand for and use of mobile devices in providing healthcare services.

These devices can present one of the biggest risks, from a compliance perspective, simply because they are mobile. They are easy to lose, easy to steal, and, in some cases, easy to hack. In the past, the issues were primarily with patient data stored on a device that was lost or stolen and providers sending unencrypted texts or emails that included patient data. Now, how-ever, mobile devices have apps that track and report patient information, apps that manage telehealth and medical appointments, and apps that coordinate care, communicate with implanted devices, and much more. Their risk exposure is enormous.

Regulatory Oversight of Healthcare Apps: Health and Human Ser-vices for apps used by, or created for, HIPAA Covered Entities; FDA for medical devices. The FTC could also be involved in cybersecurity violations or unfair and deceptive trade practices.

Compliance Brief: Protecting Those Mobile Devices

Mobile devices are at risk for theft, loss, and hacking. With workers, providers, and patients all using these devices, what can be done to min-imize risk?

One of the first things to consider is who owns the device. If a company issues devices to employees, it can exercise much greater control over the devices. Providing devices for employees and providers is a win-win: employees are happy not to use their own devices for work, and the company can control the security features and usage of the devices. The flip side is that the company must take the necessary steps to ensure the devices are compliant with HIPAA and any other applicable laws and regulations.

When mobile devices are in the hands of a company's workforce, including providers, the company must make sure it has the appropriate policies, procedures, and training in place to protect the organization and its patients. This includes not only technical security measures but also physical security.

What are the specific actions an employer or healthcare organization should take? Here are some of the key steps:

- *Provide all employees and contractors with robust HIPAA Privacy and Security training.* Include the company's specific requirements for mobile devices and give employees examples that are relatable.
- *Draft a policy and procedures for handling mobile devices.* Whether the devices are provided by the company or are employees' own personal devices, certain safeguards must be installed on the devices, and employees must handle devices with physical security in mind if they use them to view, store, or transmit any confidential information.
- *Encrypt text messages.* Text encryption is an option if providers need to share patient information via texting, and encryption generally should be a requirement.
- *Establish physical security processes for devices that are used on-site and that should not be removed.* Where are they stored? Who has access?
- *Include devices in your Security Risk Assessment.* All devices that might have PHI on them need to be evaluated.
- *Keep accurate and up-to-date records of all company-issued mobile devices.* Know where they are, who has them, and what security measures are in place. This includes software updates, patches,

and so forth that help protect the device from cyberattacks.

All this is fine for provider-controlled devices, but what about patients' devices? What is the provider's risk exposure if a patient misuses their own device or fails to secure it?

Intuitively, you might assume that this is the patient's risk, but it is not that cut and dried. If they provide an app or portal that patients can use to access PHI, providers must make sure, for instance, that all the appropriate safeguards are in place. Providers should avoid recommending apps or devices that are not HIPAA-compliant or that have a history of data breaches or misuse of patient data. Some of the cases in this book highlight how that can play out, but it's also an evolving world, so it's important to think through how patients may use any tool, app, or device in conjunction with healthcare practices and medical record systems and to consider the safety record of the companies selling them.

One More Thing: Trackers

There is one loophole that both HHS and FTC have worked to address: the use of trackers that share a user's personal information with various Big Tech companies, such as Google and Facebook, which use it for targeted advertising, for example.

Many of us have experienced some version of trackers following our movement online. We do a Google search for, as an example, a walk-in bathtub (this actually happened to me), and an hour later when we're on Facebook, ads for walk-in tubs pop up in our feed. We don't necessarily like it, but we don't know what to do about it. We know technology is tracking us online and off and sharing that information.

In healthcare, this happens when, for instance, an individual accesses a website or app in order to find a provider, treatment option, or medication. The person fills out a form with their personal information, which might include very detailed and sensitive information such as drug use history, reproductive issues, or mental health problems. The individual believes they are working with a healthcare organization and that any disclosures are protected. Some websites even claim that their software is HIPAA-compliant. But often, such information-collection sites are run by nonregulated companies that collate and distribute user information not only to the providers and suppliers that can address the individual's concerns but also to Big Tech via a pipeline.

Case in Point: Sharing Data with Big Tech

In December 2022, *The Markup* posted an article detailing an investigation into the practice of sharing data with various Big Tech companies without patients' consent.[9] I strongly recommend reading it if you are interested in this topic. Some key points are as follows:

- In October and November 2022, STAT and *The Markup* signed up for accounts and completed onboarding forms on 50 telehealth sites using a fictional identity with dummy email and social media accounts. To determine what data was being shared by the telehealth sites as they completed their forms, they examined the network traffic between trackers using Chrome DevTools, a tool built into Google's Chrome browser.
- They found Google trackers on 49 of the 50 telehealth sites and Facebook trackers on 44. Many other sites, such as Bing, TikTok, and Snapchat, also had trackers.
- Most of these telehealth companies are not regulated entities, but their tactics may rise to the level of unfair trade practices (FTC territory).
- Without updated laws and regulations, experts said that patients are left to the whims of rapidly evolving telehealth companies and tech platforms, which may choose to change their privacy policies or alter their trackers at any time.

As I've said before, the regulations haven't caught up with the technology, particularly in the healthcare space, where data is so personal but also so valuable that many industry players are looking for ways to acquire and use it.

As consumers, we can see that we need to be very judicious in what we share, or even search for, online. But what should companies that collect patient data be aware of? The FTC, not surprisingly, has put its stake in the ground:

- **Sensitive data is protected by numerous federal and state laws.** There are numerous state and federal laws that govern the collection, use, and sharing of sensitive consumer data, including many enforced by the Commission. The FTC has brought hundreds of cases to protect the security and privacy of consumers' personal information, some of which have included substantial civil penalties. In addition to Section 5 of the FTCA, which broadly prohibits unfair and deceptive trade practices, the Commission also enforces the Safeguards Rule [a HIPAA-esque rule for financial institutions], the Health Breach Notification Rule, and the Children's Online Privacy Protection Rule.

- **Claims that data is "anonymous" or "has been anonymized" are often deceptive.** Companies may try to placate consumers' privacy concerns by claiming they anonymize or aggregate data. Firms making claims about anonymization should be on guard that these claims can be a deceptive trade practice and violate the FTC Act when untrue. Significant research has shown that "anonymized" data can often be re-identified, especially in the context of location data. One set of researchers demonstrated that, in some instances, it was possible to uniquely identify 95% of a dataset of 1.5 million individuals using four location points with timestamps. Companies that make false claims about anonymization can expect to hear from the FTC.

- **The FTC cracks down on companies that misuse consumers' data.** As recent cases have shown, the FTC does not tolerate companies that over-collect, indefinitely retain, or misuse consumer data. Ad exchange OpenX recently paid $2 million for collecting children's location data without parental consent. The Commission also took action against Kurbo/Weight Watchers for, among other things, indefinitely retaining sensitive consumer data. The settlement requires the company to pay a $1.5 million fine for violating COPPA [Children's Online Privacy Protection Act], delete all illegally collected data, and also delete any work product algorithms created using that data. Just a few weeks ago, the Commission entered a final order requiring CafePress to pay redress and minimize its data collection because, according to the Commission's complaint, it improperly collected and retained consumer data, and failed to respect consumers' deletion requests, among other things.[10]

From a regulatory perspective, the web of technology, constantly emerging tools, and a vast variety of users with various agendas have created a complex situation. One of the biggest challenges to enforcement is the fact that many of the companies developing or selling medical devices or services aren't actually regulated by HIPAA. The FTC is making novel use of the FTCA by designating various cybersecurity and healthcare technology practices as "unfair or deceptive," which allows the commission to pursue practices that negatively affect individuals.

Also, as you will see, the fraud and abuse laws are being polished up and used in novel ways. Start-up companies in the health tech space need to be mindful of the many healthcare-related laws that apply (or could be interpreted to apply) to the products or services they are developing.

Telehealth and Virtual Care

The use of telehealth services has surged since the COVID pandemic. One of the first things to happen to facilitate this change was CMS including telehealth services for reimbursement. Whereas telehealth services in the past were reimbursed only under very limited circumstances, COVID created an undeniable and immediate need for patients to have remote access to care.

Although at first telehealth services were adopted by brick-and-mortar practices to accommodate patient needs, now entire practices are built around this model. The Digital Medical Society (DiMe) and American

Telemedicine Association (ATA), for instance, exist to support and promote this new care model.

The terms *telehealth* and *telemedicine* are widely used. To start with, let's define the various components of telehealth. HHS recognizes two main categories of telehealth:

Synchronous care is a live interaction between a provider and a patient. Visits may also include a caregiver, as appropriate.[11] Examples include:

- Video calls between a patient and a healthcare provider
- Audio-only calls when a video visit is not an option
- Secure text messaging to answer patient questions

Asynchronous care, also called "store and forward," is communication or information sharing among providers, patients, and caregivers that occurs at different times.[12] Examples include:

- Messaging follow-up instructions or confirmations
- Images sent for evaluation
- Lab results or vital statistics transmitted electronically

Telehealth in the Post-COVID World

During the COVID pandemic, telehealth visits accounted for up to 13 percent of all private medical claims.[13] Even though the COVID pandemic public health emergency (PHE) was officially taken off the books in May 2023, there are many sound reasons why telehealth will not only continue as a care option but also expand.

For patients who have limited transportation or mobility challenges, telehealth services can be a lifesaving alternative. Behavioral health services delivered remotely are more accessible for underserved populations and allow for easier check-ins for medication management and other follow-up care. Psychotherapy can be conducted on-screen, still face-to-face, but without as much commute time and expense. Follow-up care in general can be streamlined for patients just checking in after a medication change or procedure and for those who need to discuss a lab or imaging result.

All of these activities, in the past, usually entailed an office visit. From a patient's perspective, I might spend an hour in the car, then additional time in the waiting room, and even more in the exam room before having a five-minute consult. Spending those five minutes, instead, on a virtual visit saves everyone time. If I'm at home, the provider can call me when they are ready and I can go about my day before and after with minimal interruption.

Telehealth enables providers to run a leaner organization with more flexible hours. They can better structure their time, thereby maximizing their productivity and patient care. The patients who truly need in-person care can receive it where and when it's necessary, but those many other sorts of visits can be greatly reduced by taking care of them remotely. Last, but in no way least, remote care minimizes the spread of disease and can help keep immune-compromised, vulnerable, and elderly patients safer.

Many providers, and particularly those providers and organizations that champion the telehealth model, questioned what would happen after the PHE ended. Congress, in December 2022, put the issue to rest for the short term by amending the Social Security Act to extend the telehealth benefit under Medicare for two years. Also, permanent changes have been implemented in the field. Chapter 9 provides the details on the current regulatory framework for telehealth services under Medicare as well as an overview of the steps necessary to build a telehealth practice.

Telehealth practices, because they provide healthcare services and use health technology, need to be aware of HIPAA, of course, but also the regulations applicable to the electronic tools they employ in their practices. Review Chapter 6 on fraud and abuse as well as Chapters 3 through 5 on HHS, FDA, and FTC to be sure you fully understand all the legal and regulatory requirements that could create risk for a telehealth practice. For a more complete discussion of building a telehealth practice, see Chapter 9.

Artificial Intelligence and Machine Learning

AI is possibly the hottest topic in healthcare today, at least within the realm of healthcare technology. Although AI is already in use, this is a huge developing area and has the potential to transform healthcare. For instance, AI can be used in radiology to read X-rays and detect anomalies much faster than humans can. AI can synthesize millions of patient records to predict disease and identify options for treatment. AI can increase efficiency in scheduling care, coordinating care, consolidating and evaluating disparate health records to identify trends or potential diagnoses, and predicting care needs through predictive modeling.

The range of uses for AI is virtually limitless, but as with any technological tool, and particularly tools used in healthcare, it's critical to make sure that AI is safe, effective, and not misused. It isn't difficult to imagine a world in which AI is used to read radiology films and becomes so good at it that a physician, already pressed for time and overburdened, just goes with the machine's recommendation without adequately reviewing it for accuracy.

From a traditional healthcare compliance perspective, some obvious questions arise with respect to using AI in patient care. How is it billed? Are patients given notice? Do they consent? What quality reviews are in place?

And there are larger questions around the AI tools and technologies themselves. How are they approved and developed? What data is used to "teach" the system? Is that data representative of the entire patient population? Are biases in the original data baked in to the AI algorithms? How reliable are the results across different demographics? What about privacy? Do patients know their data is being used to "train" AI? And who is liable when something done by AI goes wrong?

Much of the emerging regulatory framework for AI comes from the FDA, which is regulating many AI-powered tools as medical devices. If you spend any time on the FDA and other related sites, you will see this referred to as Software as a Medical Device (SaMD). FDA categorizes the algorithms into two types: "Locked" algorithms incorporate data and decision-making made prior to FDA approval and then do not change or constantly incorporate new data. "Adaptive" algorithms continue learning and changing over time.

Evaluating adaptive algorithms is more challenging for the FDA, which is working on a way to categorize, review, and monitor such programs that continue adapting over time. Adaptive tools, which are highly autonomous and constantly changing, require a different review process, one that looks at the total life cycle of the product as opposed to a snapshot on the front end, as locked algorithms provide.

When we discuss AI, it's important to agree on definition of terms. The FDA uses the following terms:

> *Artificial Intelligence* has been broadly defined as the science and engineering of making intelligent machines, especially intelligent computer programs. . . . Artificial intelligence can use different techniques, including models based on statistical analysis of data, expert systems that primarily rely on if-then statements, and machine learning.
>
> *Machine Learning* is an artificial intelligence technique that can be used to design and train software algorithms to learn from and act on data. Software developers can use machine learning to create an algorithm that is "locked" so that its function does not change, or "adaptive" so its behavior can change over time based on new data.
>
> Some real-world examples of artificial intelligence and machine learning technologies include:
>
> - An imaging system that uses algorithms to give diagnostic information for skin cancer in patients.
> - A smart sensor device that estimates the probability of a heart attack.[14]

As I've noted before, the regulatory environment is struggling to keep pace with the rapid advances in healthcare technology. Nowhere is that more true than with AI. As stated by the FDA:

> "The traditional paradigm of medical device regulation was not designed for adaptive AI/ML [machine learning] technologies, which have the potential to adapt and optimize device performance

23

in real-time to continuously improve healthcare for patients. The highly iterative, autonomous, and adaptive nature of these tools requires a new, total product lifecycle (TPLC) regulatory approach that facilitates a rapid cycle of product improvement and allows these devices to continually improve while providing effective safeguards.[15]"

Not to be outdone, the FTC also has its eyes on advances in AI. FTC created an Office of Technology to support its enforcement actions. In a recent joint statement, the FTC chair joined the Civil Rights Division of the US Department of Justice, the Consumer Financial Protection Bureau, and the US Equal Employment Opportunity Commission to affirm their commitment to enforcing their respective laws and regulations that promote responsible innovation in automated systems. Although these agencies have not penned any new regulations, they are all working to apply existing laws and principles to the potential risks posed by new technologies. The FTC also has a tool for app developers that guides them on which laws apply based on the situation. The tool, and great additional information, can be found at Mobile Health App Interactive Tool on the Federal Trade Commission site (ftc.gov).

The White House has also taken action. On October 30, 2023, President Biden issued the Executive Order on the Safe, Secure, and Trustworthy Development and Use of Artificial Intelligence.[16] This EO calls on the federal government to enact and enforce protections against AI-related harms "in critical fields like healthcare, financial services, education, housing, law, and transportation," while promoting responsible uses of AI.[17]

In a follow-up six months later, on April 29, 2024, President Biden provided a comprehensive update on the progress. Note that this work crosses many industries and agencies, not just healthcare, but the document does provide a very solid road map for all the various agencies and their efforts. I recommend visiting the Whitehouse.gov website and reviewing these activities to get a better understanding of the breadth and depth of the work underway.

Most of the agency activities included in this book preceded this EO, although a few are newer. For instance, the US Patent and Trademark Office (USPTO) published guidance on April 11, 2024, to provide direction in cases where AI is used to prepare and prosecute patent and trademark applications. The USPTO emphasizes the importance of validating AI-generated documents, certification, and disclosure requirements and the need for signatures on specific documents. In other words, don't let AI do all the work and then submit applications without reviewing and confirming their accuracy. If you are involved in patent or trademark applications and are using AI for any part of that process, be sure to check the USPTO website.[18]

Meanwhile, the European Union has been hard at work tackling AI-related issues. The Artificial Intelligence Act, proposed on April 21, 2021, was approved by an overwhelming majority of the European Commission's Internal Market and Civil Liberties Committee. Its goal is to strengthen rules around data quality, transparency, human oversight, and accountability. The act is also intended to address ethical and implementation challenges that are already arising in certain sectors such as healthcare, finance, and energy.

The preface to the Eastern European's Artificial Intelligence Act states:

"Artificial Intelligence (AI) is a fast-evolving family of technologies that can bring a wide array of economic and societal benefits across the entire spectrum of industries and social activities. By improving prediction, optimizing operations and resource allocation, and personalizing service delivery, the use of artificial intelligence can support socially and environmentally beneficial outcomes and provide key competitive advantages to companies and the European economy. Such action is especially needed in high-impact sectors, including climate change, environment and health, the public sector, finance, mobility, home affairs and agriculture. However, the same elements and techniques that power the socio-economic benefits of AI can also bring about new risks or negative consequences for individuals or the society. In light of the speed of technological change and possible challenges, the EU is committed to strive for a balanced approach. It is in the Union interest to preserve the EU's technological leadership and to ensure that Europeans can benefit from new technologies developed and functioning according to Union values, fundamental rights and principles.[19]"

Here is a description of how the act will be implemented:

"The cornerstone of the AI Act is a classification system that determines the level of risk an AI technology could pose to the health and safety or fundamental rights of a person. The framework includes four risk tiers: unacceptable, high, limited and minimal.

AI systems with limited and minimal risk—like spam filters or video games—are allowed to be used with little requirements other than transparency obligations. Systems deemed to pose an unacceptable risk—like government social scoring and real-time biometric identification systems in public spaces—are prohibited with little exception.

High-risk AI systems are permitted, but developers and users must adhere to regulations that require rigorous testing, proper documentation of data quality and an accountability framework that details human oversight. AI deemed high risk include autonomous vehicles, medical devices and critical infrastructure machinery, to name a few.

The proposed legislation also outlines regulations around so-called general purpose AI, which are AI systems that can be used for different purposes with varying degrees of risk. Such technologies include, for example, large language model generative AI systems like ChatGPT.[20]"

Because of the nature of AI, such regulation clearly has a worldwide impact because entry into the EU internal market would require conformity with the final standards. It is likely that, once such standards are finalized, they would become more broadly accepted and adopted to facilitate a consistent framework for regulating and monitoring AI. Agency lawmaking in the United States must be mindful of these developments because AI and health tech cross time and space boundaries and will be a morass of confusion without due diligence and coordination with other markets.

Although this act has made significant progress and is certainly leading the world in terms of regulating AI, it must go through additional steps, including European Parliamentary adoption of a position and subsequent lengthy EU interinstitutional negotiation on final rules.

There are, however, already areas of concern. One big challenge is creating AI algorithms that can make use of multiple software and systems. When hospitals, practices, and healthcare organizations all use different software and processes, it's difficult to create AI that can consolidate the dissimilar data sets into one repository and then perform meaningful analysis. As a result, hospitals and health systems that have the resources may develop their own AI algorithms. These homegrown AI systems are not subject to FDA oversight and therefore no consistent standards are in place. Privacy and security measures may not be adequate, for instance, or the data may not be sufficient for useful and accurate analysis because an organization's data set may not represent all segments of the patient population, which can lead to distorted or discriminatory outcomes.

Compliance Brief: What to Do About AI

The emergence of AI as an issue for healthcare organizations reminds me of the challenge our industry faced when social media became an issue. How do we control use, and to what degree should we? How can we use it to our advantage? How can we keep our employees from misusing it or exposing our organization to risk? These are all valid questions—industry standards are yet to emerge. AI, however, has a much larger potential impact on patient care, so it is vital for healthcare organizations to monitor standards development in this landscape and, when appropriate, embrace them. Looking ahead, the possibilities of AI in conjunction with new models of care, such as value-based care, for instance, provide a bright glimpse into what the future of healthcare might look like if we approach this evolution with deliberate thoughtfulness.

I have a few suggestions on how you can begin to protect your organization as AI tools proliferate in the healthcare industry.

1. **Keep existing laws and regulations in mind.** Privacy and security of patient and other confidential information are still critical. Information fed into "open AI" cannot be retrieved, so don't put patient data out there, for instance, to get a diagnostic opinion. That might sound obvious, but do all your employees understand this principle? As people become

more comfortable using AI tools, privacy and security will become greater risks.

- **To do:** First, identify the various ways AI is being used or may be used in your organization or practice as best you can (in very large organizations, this can be a project all by itself, so you will likely need a committee or other assistance).
- I recommend conducting a risk assessment of the various AI uses, the controls in place, and the risk areas needing attention based on priority/risk levels and the various applicable laws, as outlined in this book or as enacted going forward.
- Review your employee educational content and policies related to the use and disclosure of confidential information. Update policies and training materials to address AI-related uses and disclosures, such as the use of ChatGPT. Update your HIPAA Notice of Privacy Practices if applicable.

2. **Address internal AI tools and processes.** If you are part of a large organization, is your department developing its own AI processes using existing patient data? If so, keep in mind appropriate uses of that data, as referenced in the first point above. Is machine learning considered research? Development? Or could you call it "operations" under HIPAA as an acceptable use without authorization?

- **To do:** If you are involved in developing AI, review which information is being used and where it comes from. You might be able to make the argument that this use of patient information—if strictly internal—is "healthcare operations" under HIPAA. If that is the case, then update your Notice of Privacy Practices accordingly.
- Have patients agreed to the data usage? Because this is a developing regulatory field, it's best to err on the side of protecting patient rights and privacy, even if regulatory loopholes might currently exist. Also, keep in mind that for matters not directly specified in laws or regulations, it is acceptable to establish your own policy that conforms with the spirit of the laws.

- This is important to keep in mind as our regulations and agency guidance continue to evolve. If you make a decision in the absence of a legal standard, be sure to document the rationale; get feedback from key stakeholders such as your attorney, compliance officer, and IT staff; and create a policy and communication plan to make sure employees understand the organization's expectations. The main idea here is to make sure you can explain and defend your position if ever called on to do so. Do stay informed of emerging regulatory standards because they could impact your policy decisions.

3. **Consider patient consent.** Is AI playing any role in diagnosis or treatment? Patients should be informed if so, and their consent must be sought.

- **To do:** Review any use of AI in diagnosis or treatment and update your consent documents accordingly.

4. **Put in place data use agreements.** What do your current contracts say about data sharing? Where does your data go and what do those organizations do with it? It's time to revisit this question in light of business partners who may be using or developing AI tools.

- **To do:** Review all the channels where your data flows and who your vendors and business associates are. Are any of them involved in, or owned by, companies developing healthcare AI tools? Ask your business partners these questions and reconsider your arrangements (or update your agreements) if your data is being used outside of the intended scope.

- This is a good step to take in any situation because of the proliferation of electronic data sharing. It's easy to lose track of what data is going where. Consider mapping this and revisiting/updating regularly. If a breach occurs, you will be glad you did.

- Keep in mind that patient healthcare data is an increasingly valuable commodity that does have a dollar value on the black market. It is also used for marketing and other activities, so review any agreements with business partners to make sure you are satisfied with how they can use or disclose your data.

Conclusion

As you can see, there are many types of healthcare technology. They vary in terms of how much they interact with a patient, how much patient information they contain or transmit, and how they are regulated. The COVID pandemic forced some fast changes from HHS and CMS, such as expanding the coverage of telehealth services and allowing more flexibility in certain HIPAA requirements, but those were very specific changes and were not considered permanent, although that may be changing.

It's also not entirely clear how healthcare technology should be regulated. Is there one agency that should "own" the oversight of health tech? Should it be the Federal Trade Commission? Health and Human Services? The Food and Drug Administration? Right now, they all address some aspects of healthcare technology, which I outline in this book. But all this is very much subject to change, just like the technology itself is likely to continue to evolve at a rapid rate.

Even during the process of writing this book, things are changing. Every time I check an agency's website, there is a new notice, proposed rule, or enforcement action! Keep in mind, also, that this book is focused on US laws, but the rest of the world is working on this issue as well, so this complex topic will continue to develop from the regulatory standpoint.

In the next chapter, I provide details on the key laws and regulatory agencies that have a role in regulating health tech.

PART II
The Current Regulatory Framework

CHAPTER 2
Health and Human Services: HIPAA

Who Needs to Read This: All healthcare providers and their Business Associates; anyone providing services or technology to healthcare providers or other HIPAA Covered Entities who uses, transmits, discloses, or stores Protected Health Information, including digital healthcare developers and vendors.

Not surprisingly, Health and Human Services (HHS) is front and center in regulating key aspects of healthcare technology. That being said, the laws are struggling to keep up with technology, and the current challenge is how to apply the principles and requirements to technologies that did not exist, or that were not in common use, when the regulations were put into place. When the Health Insurance Portability and Accountability Act of 1996 (HIPAA) became law (for those of us old enough to remember the painful implementation), many health claims and transactions were still paper-based, as were many medical records. "Standard transactions" and "interoperability" weren't in common parlance, and certainly "AI" wasn't part of our daily nomenclature.

For this chapter, I'm focusing on the sections of the HIPAA regulations and the Cures Act that most likely impact tech-based healthcare services. This is not intended to be a comprehensive discussion of all HIPAA requirements that exist. Numerous other books, as well as online resources such as the Health and Human Services website (hhs.gov), focus on HIPAA for anyone wanting that level of detail. In this chapter, I will also touch on the guidance issued by the Agency for Healthcare Research and Quality

(AHRQ). Also, keep in mind that the Office of Civil Rights (OCR) enforces the Privacy Rule.

HIPAA

When health tech companies reference compliance, it's often the Health Insurance Portability and Accountability Act of 1996 that they are primarily thinking of. It's important to understand both what the regulations include and how they apply to the different types of organizations and healthcare technologies.

HIPAA, for our purposes, includes the Privacy Rule, the Security Rule, and the Breach Notification Rule. We will go over each of them but will start with some basic definitions that may help you define your organization's role within the HIPAA framework.

Key Terms and Definitions

A lot of times the questions around applicability can be answered by a close read of the definitions, so I've included some of the key terms here, as outlined in the Health Insurance Portability and Accountability Act of 1996.[21]

Covered Entity

A Covered Entity is:

1. A healthcare provider who transmits any information in an electronic form in connection with a transaction for which HHS has adopted a standard, or
1. A health plan (including private plans, HMOs, and government payers), or
1. A healthcare clearinghouse.

Breach

A Breach is defined as:

The unauthorized acquisition, access, use, or disclosure of protected health information which compromises the security or privacy of such information, except where an unauthorized person to whom such information is disclosed would not reasonable have been able to retain such information.

The Breach Notification Rule further clarifies what is meant by "compromises the security or privacy of such information" as "poses a significant risk of financial, reputational, or other harm to the individual."

Business Associate

A Business Associate is defined as:

1. Except as provided in paragraph (4) of this definition, business associate means, with respect to a covered entity, a person who:

(i) On behalf of such covered entity or of an organized health care arrangement (as defined in this section) in which the covered entity participates, but other than in the capacity of a member of the workforce of such covered entity or arrangement, creates, receives, maintains, or transmits protected health information for a function or activity regulated by this subchapter, including claims processing or administration, data analysis, processing or administration, utilization review, quality assurance, patient safety activities listed at 42 CFR 3.20, billing, benefit management, practice management, and repricing; or

(ii) Provides, other than in the capacity of a member of the workforce of such covered entity, legal, actuarial, accounting, consulting, data aggregation (as defined in ⊠ 164.501 of this subchapter), management, administrative, accreditation, or financial services to or for such covered entity, or to or for an organized health care arrangement in which the covered entity participates, where the provision of the service involves the disclosure of protected health information from such covered entity or arrangement, or from another business associate of such covered entity or arrangement, to the person.

2. A covered entity may be a business associate of another covered entity.
3. Business associate includes:

(i) A Health Information Organization, E-prescribing Gateway, or other person that provides data transmission services with respect to protected health information to a covered entity and that requires access on a routine basis to such protected health information.

(ii) A person that offers a personal health record to one or more individuals on behalf of a covered entity.

(iii) A subcontractor that creates, receives, maintains, or transmits protected health information on behalf of the business associate.

4. Business associate does not include:

(i) A health care provider, with respect to disclosures by a covered entity to the health care provider concerning the treatment of the individual.

(ii) A plan sponsor, with respect to disclosures by a group health plan (or by a health insurance issuer or HMO with respect to a group health plan) to the plan sponsor, to the extent that the requirements of § 164.504(f) of this subchapter apply and are met.

(iii) A government agency, with respect to determining eligibility for, or enrollment in, a government health plan that provides public benefits and is administered by another government agency, or collecting protected health information for such purposes, to the extent such activities are authorized by law.

(iv) A covered entity participating in an organized health care arrangement that performs a function or activity as described by paragraph (1)(i) of this definition for or on behalf of such organized health care arrangement, or that provides a service as described in paragraph (1)(ii) of this definition to or for such organized health care arrangement by virtue of such activities or services

Who is a Business Associate? Often, you can answer this easily by thinking through the definition. For example:

1. *Is your organization using and disclosing PHI?* If so, you're a Business Associate. But that's just the first question—don't stop there.

2. *Is your organization using or disclosing the information* on behalf of *a Covered Entity?* In other words, are you doing it on behalf of or for a physician's practice, hospital, insurance company, or healthcare clearinghouse? This one can be tricky in the world of multiple layers of technology, vendors, and different types of Covered Entities. So think about who you are providing services for. If that organization is a Covered Entity and you are using or transmitting PHI, then you are a Business Associate. In addition, if you are contracting with a Business Associate and otherwise fit the definition, you likely also are subject to the requirements because Business Associates themselves are now liable for failure to comply with HIPAA.

3. *Are you exchanging PHI solely for treatment purposes?* If you're a provider and so is the other party, then there is no Business Associate relationship—no agreement or special consent is necessary if the exchange is purely to provide treatment. Note, however, that if your organization provides other services, for instance, your office does some sort of data aggregation to evaluate quality of care as a service to the other provider, you are now entering into Business Associate territory. Be very careful in assessing the exact purpose of the exchange.

4. *Are cloud service providers (CSPs) Business Associates?* Yes. Even if the CSP doesn't actually access encrypted electronic PHI (ePHI) that it stores or transmits, it is still subject to the HIPAA Security Rule requirements. There must be a Business Associate Agreement (BAA) in place. The actual safeguards that the CSP must have in place may vary, depending on what information the Business Associate actually can access and other variables. The specific requirements for the CSP versus the Covered Entity should

be detailed in the underlying agreement. For instance, which party is responsible for access controls?

5. If the Covered Entity does not enter into a BAA with a CSP, and ePHI is being stored or transmitted by the CSP, the Covered Entity is out of compliance with the HIPAA Security Rule. CSPs must report security incidents to either the Covered Entity or Business Associate that is their client. The details in the Business Associate Agreement are particularly important in these arrangements where the different parties have responsibility and control over different aspects of security and access. It's important, no matter which party you are, to carefully review the actual service-level agreement and the BAA to ensure you are only committing to implementing the safeguards that you will have control over.

One key point about Business Associates—and this one is important for vendors to understand—ever since the Health Information Technology for Economic and Clinical Health (HITECH) Act was enacted, Business Associates are now held to the same standards as Covered Entities.[22] This means that you may be considered a Business Associate for a health plan, but when you subcontract some of your duties for the health plan to outside vendors, you are essentially standing in the shoes of the health plan, which is the Covered Entity. You will therefore need to have a Business Associate Agreement with your subcontractors if they are handling PHI.

Protected Health Information

A basic issue to understand is what constitutes Protected Health Information (PHI), because this is the data at issue and subject to the rules. The HIPAA rules apply to PHI that is used or disclosed via any medium, including oral disclosures; fax; images in phones, cameras, or copy machines; paper records; or connected devices and electronic medical records. The author of the records is not determinative.

- PHI can reside in many locations and includes the following elements:

- Names (including relatives, employers, household members)
- Geographic subdivisions smaller than a state
- All elements of dates that relate to:
  - Birth or death
  - Admissions or discharges
  - Ages over 89
- Telephone, cell phone, and fax numbers
- Social Security numbers
- Biometric identifiers, such as fingerprints
- Photos (full face or image that would render patient recognizable)
- Medical record number
- Health plan or subscriber identification number
- Account numbers
- Certificate or license numbers
- Vehicle identifiers
- Email and website addresses
- Any other unique identifying data

The Privacy Rule

The HIPAA Privacy requirements are less related to technical IT security components and more in line with administrative controls. This does not mean that the penalties are less onerous or enforcement softer. Under the HIPAA Privacy Rule, organizations are frequently penalized for issues like failing to provide patients with access to their medical records or not providing a "Notice of Privacy Practices."

Breaches often include violations of both the Privacy Rule and the Security Rule. If you are a virtual provider, of course, you are a healthcare provider and a Covered Entity, so all the requirements apply to you.

Because every day we hear about mega security breaches, it's easy to forget about basic HIPAA Privacy Rule requirements. But even if you forget, Health and Human Services does not.

Case in Point: Optum Health

Optum Health isn't the biggest settlement you'll see. It entered into a Resolution Agreement with HHS that included, in part, payment of $160,000 and a mandatory Corrective Action Plan (CAP).[23] This case is just an example of how an organization can come under fire for failing to adhere to administrative requirements.

But what did Optum do wrong? It failed to give patients a copy of their medical records.

I mention this small case as a reminder: If you are a Covered Entity or Business Associate under HIPAA, the Privacy Rule applies to you and is being enforced. A number of cases have been based purely on violation of patient rights under HIPAA, such as in this case. And even though the dollar amount is not huge (it would be if this were a small practice), it's no fun being under a CAP. Also, penalties escalate when there's a lack of cooperation with HHS—I've seen that in several cases over the years.

Entire books have been written to provide guidance on HIPAA, and there are thousands of pages of government-generated regulations and guidance. My challenge here is to distill all that down to key concepts that potentially apply to a healthcare-technology-based company and the requirements it needs to have in place. The following is certainly not interpretation or application of the entire rule, so have members of your team who are well-versed in the rule review your procedures.

One of the foundations of the HIPAA Privacy Rule is the set of requirements around the use and disclosure of PHI, what is permitted and what is not. Another part addresses situations when the patient needs to authorize the release of their information and what their rights are. These are the core issues outlined in the Notice of Privacy Practices.

The Privacy Rule is specific about how organizations covered by HIPAA can use or disclose patients' PHI.[24] Your organization can use or disclose PHI in the following circumstances:

1. To the *individual* who is the subject of the information (or who is legally authorized, such as by a power of attorney).
2. *For treatment, payment, and operations.* This is a core concept, and often confused.

- Disclosures for *treatment* mean disclosing to other people or organizations that are also treating the patient. Most organizations get the patient's authorization anyway, but you are allowed to share a patient's information with other providers, with verification that they are, in fact, treating the individual.
- *Payment* disclosures are pretty straightforward: You can send records of the patient's care to the patient's insurance company to help the patient secure claims payment.
- *Operations* is a broad category, and you might want to review the numerous questions and answers/FAQ on the HHS website for further understanding.[25] For operations disclosures, think about things like quality review, legal claims/cases/attorneys, peer and utilization review, and accreditation. What are the various ways you might need to use patient data to manage your practice? Chances are those would fit into this category, which means you don't have to get a specific authorization or track or report that usage. Be careful, though. Marketing, for instance, is not one of the areas where you can share patient information without the patient authorizing that use.

3. *Incidental uses and disclosures.* These are disclosures that are a natural by-product of a permitted use or disclosure. This one is somewhat vague, but it can come up, for instance, if a patient overhears two nurses talking about a mutual patient at the nurses' station. The nurses are providing care and are coordinating that care, but another patient overhears the conversation. The disclosure from one nurse to the other was appropriate, but the nurses weren't aware of another patient within hearing distance.

4. Pursuant to, and in compliance with, a *valid authorization.* The specific requirements for an authorization to use or disclose PHI can be found at Section 164.508. Note, however, that the authorization itself can dictate specific records being released or not, so that document needs to be referenced prior to releasing records.

5. *Pursuant to an agreement* under or as otherwise permitted by Section 16.501, or in compliance with Section 164.512 or 164.514 (e), (f), or (g). These sections refer to disclosures allowed when the patient doesn't have an opportunity to agree or object and to the use of limited data sets and fundraising.

The main thing about the Privacy Rule is to thoroughly ensure everyone in your organization (or working on behalf of your organization) understands which disclosures are allowable and when you need an authorization. This is a big area of confusion and can be a huge cause of dissatisfaction for patients and, consequently, your provider clients and colleagues.

Minimum Necessary

When people are trained on the Privacy Rule, one of the core concepts for them to understand is *minimum necessary*. This is a foundational principle that requires your practice to limit the information shared to only that which the recipient truly needs. There are exceptions to this standard:

1. Disclosures to a healthcare provider for treatment
2. Disclosures to an individual (the subject of the information or their lawful representative)
3. Disclosures pursuant to an authorization
4. Disclosures to the Secretary of Health and Human Services or designee
5. Disclosures required by law

The Minimum Necessary standard is one that often, I think, gets forgotten in day-to-day operations. It is your job to keep this standard in mind if you receive a record request. Depending on the services you provide, this issue may not apply to you. But if you do manage and/or transmit PHI, the odds are that you will get such a request. Requests can come from a variety of quarters: healthcare providers, attorneys, workers' compensation carriers, government and private payers, and a variety of others who ask for all records. These entities will not necessarily follow a Minimum Necessary standard in their request—it's easier for them to just ask for everything. But it *is* your duty to release only the minimum amount, subject to the above exceptions.

When you get open-ended record requests, you are obligated to contact the requestor and ask them to narrow the scope. If, for instance, the patient hurt their back in a work accident, the workers' compensation carrier doesn't need records related to a past pregnancy. This issue can get contentious, and certainly the patient can authorize all records be released, and in some cases that's appropriate. But it is up to you to adhere to the Minimum Necessary standard and to make sure your staff also understand it and where it must be applied.

Another related area of confusion involves records your practice did not create. Those records are, indeed, part of the Designated Record Set, as defined by HIPAA, and those records should be included in any record request if they are within the scope.

Patient Rights

HIPAA defines a number of rights that patients have regarding their PHI:

- Accounting of Disclosures
- Right to Amend
- Right to Confidential Communication
- Right to Restrict Disclosures
- Right to Access

These rights should all be listed in your Notice of Privacy Practices if you are a Covered Entity and must have a notice. You should have some documented procedure in place to address them all. Some of these rights might rarely arise, but you still need a process, and staff must understand the rights and the related procedures.

Keep in mind that, if you should be audited by the government, the auditors will look over your processes to ensure patient rights are being upheld. HIPAA doesn't mandate specific processes in most cases, but you do always want to have a paper trail and make sure staff is trained on patient rights. Patients must make the above requests in writing, and your responses should be in writing as well.

The Security Rule

The HIPAA Security Rule, which applies to all Covered Entities, can be found at 45 C.F.R. Parts 160 and 164, Subparts A and C. Given the dramatic increase in the use of electronic systems and processes for managing healthcare data, and even services, information security should be top of mind for any organization using or providing electronic platforms or services in the healthcare industry.

The Security Rule provides specific protections for ePHI.[26] With the ever-increasing use of electronic devices and communications and the resulting explosion in various information security scams, ransomware attacks, malware, viruses, and so forth, the HIPAA Security Rule is increasingly critical for the protection of patients' electronic data. If you are building an app or other health tech program, consider these rules throughout the process and have a security expert involved from the beginning.

The overarching goals of the Security Rule are to protect the confidentiality, availability, and integrity of ePHI. To that end, specific requirements exist to determine what type of security is necessary to identify and protect against security threats and to periodically review security measures.

The HIPAA Security Rule has undergone changes since the original 1996 version. The HITECH Act, and then the subsequent Omnibus Final Rules changes, which went into effect September 23, 2013, strengthened the HIPAA requirements and civil monetary penalties. Not only did HITECH address privacy and security of electronic transmissions of ePHI, but it also standardized electronic health records (EHRs) and served as further impetus in the adoption of Meaningful Use of health information technology. This is the reason that HIPAA Security requirements are incorporated into Meaningful Use standards. Another significant change at this time was the imposition of direct liability on Business Associates and their subcontractors for HIPAA violations. This is why the earlier analysis of Business Associate status is so important.

One helpful aspect of the Security Rule is that it is scalable and can be adapted to different sizes and types of healthcare organizations. This is particularly important for small practices that clearly don't have the budgets of large hospitals, for instance. The Security Rule identifies the types of safeguards as administrative, physical, and technical, each with a number of associated standards.

You find, as you dig deeper into Security Rule requirements, that some of these standards are "required" and some are "addressable" to identify and protect against security threats and to periodically review security measures. As a result, specific technologies are not required, but you do need to document your assessment of the risks. In addition, your security team needs to understand which related state laws are applicable to your organization. In the world of virtual care, this may not be so simple to determine; if this is the case, your best bet is to seek guidance from an attorney who specializes in the privacy and security laws and regulations.

The Security Risk Assessment (SRA) is a key foundational requirement for all Covered Entities (and, by extension, Business Associates) under the Security Rule. This requirement is also included in Meaningful Use standards and is an annual requirement. This risk assessment is basically an evaluation of each standard under the Security Rule as it is in effect (or not) at your organization.

You will see that the Security Rule includes administrative, physical, and technical safeguard requirements that apply to Covered Entities and Business Associates who create, receive, maintain, or transmit ePHI. I provide a summary of each below, along with the recommended steps to take.

Note which are *required* and which are *addressable*. For any standard you decide not to meet or that doesn't apply, be sure your rationale is documented. The following standards are taken directly from the Security Rule, but the to-do items are my recommendations, not guidance from the government.

Administrative Safeguards

1. **Security Management Process (Required).** "Implement policies and procedures to prevent, detect, contain, and correct security violations."

   a. **Risk Analysis (Required).** "Conduct an accurate and thorough assessment of the potential risks and vulnerabilities to the confidentiality, integrity, and availability of electronic protected health information held by the covered entity."

To do: Identify all the ePHI in your organization, whether it's being created, received, maintained, or transmitted. ePHI can appear on any type of device, server, or workstation. Think of everything here—printers, implantable devices, and so forth . . . certain items are frequently missed.

b. Risk Management (Required). "Implement security measures sufficient to reduce risks and vulnerabilities to a reasonable and appropriate level to comply with 164.306 (a)."

To do: This is the outgrowth of the risk analysis and includes evaluating and addressing all manner of administrative, physical, or technical security measures in place to protect ePHI.

c. Sanction Policy (Required). This is a HIPAA requirement but also an expected element of a compliance program. This policy serves to outline "appropriate sanctions against workforce members who fail to comply with the security policies and procedures of the covered entity."

To do: Develop a sanctions policy that describes corrective actions to be taken for workforce members who violate the organization's security policies and procedures. This policy can be combined with the more general compliance sanctions policy, so I provide greater detail in Chapter 8, "Compliance Programs for Health Tech Companies."

2. Workforce Security. "Implement policies and procedures to ensure that all members of [your] workforce have appropriate access to electronic protected health information, and to prevent those workforce members who do not have access from obtaining access to electronic protected health information."

a. Authorization and/or Supervision (Addressable). "Implement procedures for the authorization and/or supervision of workforce members wo work with ePHI or in locations where it might be accessed."

To do: Check your procedures to ensure that only the people who need access to ePHI have such access. This is not always as simple a determination as you might think, when you stop to consider various vendors and their workforces. How do you ensure all individuals have the access they need and no more? How do you ensure that a Business Associate will properly terminate an employee's access when appropriate?

3. **Security Awareness and Training.** "Implement a security awareness and training program for all members of the workforce (including management)."

    a. **Password Management (Addressable).** "Implement procedures for creating, changing, and safeguarding passwords."

    To do: Train your workforce not to share passwords and to keep passwords in a secure location. Consider creating a policy that requires passwords routinely be changed.

4. **Contingency Plan.** "Establish (and implement as needed) policies and procedures for responding to an emergency or other occurrence (for example, fire, vandalism, system failure, and natural disaster) that damages systems that contain electronic protected health information."

    a. **Data Backup Plan (Required).** "Establish and implement procedures to create and maintain retrievable exact copies of electronic protected health information."

    To do: Make sure you have procedures that identify all sources of ePHI that must be backed up, including medical records, patient accounting systems, electronic test results, orders, and diagnostic test results, and a process for consistently and reliably backing that data up.

5. **Business Associate Contracts and Other Arrangements.** "A covered entity may permit a Business Associate to create, receive, maintain, or transmit electronic protected health information on the covered entity's behalf only if the covered entity obtains satisfactory assurances that the Business Associate will appropriately safeguard the information."

a. Written Contract or Other Arrangements (Required).
"Document the satisfactory assurances required by this section through a written contract or other arrangement with the Business Associate that meets the applicable requirements of 164.314(a)."

To do: This is one of the most important administrative requirements for health tech start-ups, in my opinion, because data is likely a very big piece of your business, whether that's transmitting it, storing it, or using it to enhance services. The Business Associate Agreement must define how the data may be used and shared. Keep in mind, data has value in today's market, much more so than when HIPAA was originally drafted. Whether you are a Covered Entity or a Business Associate, make sure an agreement defines with specificity which data is being shared, how, and which protections will be in place.

Another critical aspect is managing breaches. The BAA needs to address breach notification expectations. If a Business Associate has a breach, how long before the Covered Entity must be notified? Who notifies patients once a risk assessment is completed? These are the types of issues that can create a nightmare if not addressed up front. Also, read the previous section on the HIPAA Privacy Rule for more details on Business Associates.

Physical Safeguards

1. **Facility Access Controls.** "Implement policies and proce-dures to limit physical access to [your] electronic informa-tion systems and the facility or facilities in which they are housed, while ensuring that properly authorized access is allowed."

    a. Facility Security Plan (Addressable). "Implement policies and procedures to safeguard the facility and the equipment therein from unauthorized physical access, tam-pering, and theft."

To do: Do you have policies and procedures to secure your ePHI from theft and tampering? Think of security measures as simple as locked areas, surveillance cameras, and physical security measures for various devices. This is another one that can be trickier than it appears: If you have a remote workforce, for instance, how is data kept secure? If you have various vendors providing key components of your service, how are they securing your data?

b. Maintenance Records (Addressable). "Implement policies and procedures to document repairs and modification to the physical components of a facility which are related to security (for example hardware, walls, doors, and locks)."

To do: This one is pretty straightforward: Keep records of the repairs or maintenance of any aspect of a facility that relates to securing your data.

2. **Workstation Use (Required).** "Implement policies and procedures that specify the proper functions to be performed, the manner in which those functions are to be performed, and the physical attributes of the surroundings of a specific workstation or class of workstations that can access electronic protected health information."

   To do: No applicable standard, but the to-do list includes workstation privacy and security measures such as privacy screens, logoff procedures, and time-outs. Another common issue comes up around the use of shared workstations and password sharing, both of which must be addressed.

3. **Device and Media Controls.** "Implement policies and procedures that govern the receipt and removal of hardware and electronic media that contain ePHI into and out of a facility, and the movement of these items within a facility."

   a. Disposal (Required): "Implement policies and procedures to address the final disposition of electronic protected health information, and/or the hardware or electronic media on which it is stored."

   To do: Make sure you have a consistent and documented

process for disposal and think about it carefully, including where your data might reside and who might need to destroy it (it might not be you or your organization). Make sure your vendors have procedures in place consistent with your policies and that they are following them. In the event of a breach, a failure to have destroyed data can exponentially increase your risk and exposure.

b. Data Backup and Storage (Addressable). "Create a retrievable, exact copy of electronic protected health information, when needed, before movement of equipment."

To do: As noted before, make sure you have a process to ensure an exact copy of data is retrievable.

4. **Access Controls.** "Implement technical policies and procedures for electronic information systems that maintain electronic protected health information to allow access only to those persons or software programs that have been granted access rights as specific in 164.308(a)(4)."

a. Unique User Identification (Required). "Assign a unique name and/or number for identifying and tracking user identity."

To do: Make sure not only your employees but also any vendors with access have a unique ID that can be used to track their activity.

Technical Safeguards

1. **Person or Entity Authentication (Required).** "Implement procedures to verify that a person or entity seeking access to electronic protected health information is the one claimed."

To do: Ensure access to ePHI is granted only pursuant to password or other defined login credentialing. Review the Cures Act, Anti-Information Blocking Rule, discussed in more detail in Chapter 3.

2. **Transmission Security (Required).** "Implement technical security measures to guard against unauthorized access to electronic protected health information that is being

transmitted over an electronic communications network."

a. Encryption. "Implement a mechanism to encrypt electronic protected health information whenever deemed appropriate."

To do: Based on your risk analysis, determine whether encryption is necessary for ePHI flowing between your organization and outside entities. If not, what measures are in place to protect this data? Encryption is a standard practice now, so this requirement shouldn't be a surprise. Think about all the ways ePHI is transmitted—emails, texts, photographs, via various apps. Is the data encrypted in all of these scenarios? What about while the data is "at rest"? These are all issues to evaluate and manage.

Case in Point: Lafourche Medical

Here is a headline and announcement from the HHS website:

HHS' OFFICE FOR CIVIL RIGHTS SETTLES FIRST EVER
PHISHING CYBER-ATTACK INVESTIGATION

Louisiana Medical Group settles after investigation reveals large cyber-security breach affecting nearly 35,000 patients

Today, the US Department of Health and Human Services (HHS), Office for Civil Rights (OCR), announced a settlement with Lafourche Medical Group, a Louisiana medical group specializing in emergency medicine, occupational medicine, and laboratory testing. The settlement resolves an investigation following a phishing attack that affected the electronic protected health information of approximately 34,862 individuals. Phishing is a type of cybersecurity attack used to trick individuals into disclosing sensitive information via electronic communication, such as email, by impersonating a trustworthy source. This marks the first settlement OCR has resolved involving a phishing attack under the Health Insurance Portability and Accountability Act (HIPAA) Rules. HIPAA is the federal law that protects the privacy and security of health information.

"Phishing is the most common way that hackers gain access to health care systems to steal sensitive data and health information," said OCR Director

Melanie Fontes Rainer. "It is imperative that the health care industry be vigilant in protecting its systems and sensitive medical records, which includes regular training of staff and consistently monitoring and managing system risk to prevent these attacks. We all have a role to play in keeping our health care system safe and taking preventive steps against phishing attacks."

On May 28, 2021, Lafourche Medical Group filed a breach report with HHS stating that a hacker, through a successful phishing attack on March 30, 2021, gained access to an email account that contained electronic protected health information. When protected health information is compromised by a cyber-attack breach such as phishing, incredibly sensitive information about an individual's medical records is at risk. The types of sensitive information can include medical diagnoses, frequency of visits to a therapist or other health care professionals, and where an individual seeks medical treatment.

Phishing attacks can result in identity theft, financial loss, discrimination, stigma, mental anguish, negative consequences to the reputation, health, or physical safety of the individual or to others identified in the individual's protected health information. Health care providers, health plans and data clearinghouses regulated by HIPAA are required to file breach reports with HHS. Based on the large breaches reported to OCR this year, over 89 million individuals have been affected by large breaches. In 2022, over 55 million individuals were affected.

OCR's investigation revealed that, prior to the 2021 reported breach, Lafourche Medical Group failed to conduct a risk analysis to identify potential threats or vulnerabilities to electronic protected health information across the organization as required by HIPAA. OCR also discovered that Lafourche Medical Group had no policies or procedures in place to regularly review information system activity to safeguard protected health information against cyberattacks.

As a result, Lafourche Medical Group agreed to pay $480,000 to OCR and to implement a corrective action plan that will be monitored by OCR for two years. Lafourche Medical Group will take the following steps to resolve and comply with:

- Establishing and implementing security measures to reduce security risks and vulnerabilities to electronic protect health information

in order to keep patients' protected health information secure;
- Developing, maintaining, and revising written policies and procedures as necessary to comply with the HIPAA Rules; and
- Providing training to all staff members who have access to
patients' protected health information on HIPAA policies and
procedures."[27]

Why is this case significant? What struck me was that the healthcare organization was the *victim* of a phishing attack but ended up with a healthy fine and a Corrective Action Plan (ouch!). Another issue is that it failed to conduct the required Security Risk Assessment, which, presumably, would have identified the security gaps. This is not unusual, especially among smaller organizations or start-ups because it can be a stretch for them to hire a contractor to do the SRA or expend valuable internal resources on it (if they even have the technological skills).

But I wouldn't skip this requirement . . . if it's the only thing you do, in terms of the HIPAA Security Rule, start with the SRA.

Breach Notification Rule

According to HHS:

"A breach is, generally, an impermissible use or disclosure under the Privacy Rule that compromises the security or privacy of the protected health information. An impermissible use or disclosure of protected health information is presumed to be a breach unless the covered entity or business associate, as applicable, demonstrates that there is a low probability that the protected health information has been compromised based on a risk assessment of at least the following factors:

1. The nature and extent of the protected health information involved, including the types of identifiers and the likelihood of re-identification;
2. The unauthorized person who used the protected health information or to whom the disclosure was made;
3. Whether the protected health information was actually

acquired or viewed; and

4. The extent to which the risk to the protected health information has been mitigated.

Covered entities and business associates, where applicable, have discretion to provide the required breach notifications following an impermissible use or disclosure without performing a risk assessment to determine the probability that the protected health information has been compromised.

There are three exceptions to the definition of "breach." The first exception applies to the unintentional acquisition, access, or use of protected health information by a workforce member or person acting under the authority of a covered entity or business associate, if such acquisition, access, or use was made in good faith and within the scope of authority. The second exception applies to the inadvertent disclosure of protected health information by a person authorized to access protected health information at a covered entity or business associate to another person authorized to access protected health information at the covered entity or business associate, or organized health care arrangement in which the covered entity participates. In both cases, the information cannot be further used or disclosed in a manner not permitted by the Privacy Rule. The final exception applies if the covered entity or business associate has a good faith belief that the unauthorized person to whom the impermissible disclosure was made, would not have been able to retain the information.[28]"

In other words, a breach is any misuse of PHI, and notifications are required unless you conduct a risk assessment and determine that the actual risk is minimal. For instance, maybe an employee was curious about a patient (whose care she was not involved in) and "snooped" in the patient's record. That's obviously not appropriate or allowed under HIPAA. Depending on why the employee was accessing a record inappropriately, this may not have created sufficient risk to trigger the notification requirement.

If, however, that employee was routinely accessing records without a legitimate purpose and was using that information for personal gain, then the assessment would be different. This is why the risk assessment process is important, and you want to be sure to maintain documentation.

Note that I'm not suggesting the snooping example should be ignored—not at all. Even with something like that, where the information presumably doesn't leave the organization, it is still a violation and has to be dealt with. Depending on the facts and your policies, the employee may be terminated or may be put on a Corrective Action Plan (CAP). You might also want to review and refresh your employee education and training policies to discourage other employees from similar conduct.

Compliance Brief: Processes for Managing a Breach

The one thing you don't want to do is figure out how to handle a data breach when you're in the middle of one. Regardless of your line of business, if you handle confidential patient data, you need to have some basic processes in place to manage a breach timely.

The first thing to do is to identify the applicable laws and regulations. This is important because you might have a state law that is more stringent or has different requirements than HIPAA. Generally speaking, the more stringent rules are the ones that apply, but states can also add specific provisions you need to incorporate. For instance, they might have additional requirements you must include in breach notification letters or reporting timeframes. Gathering this information is your first stop, and if you're not comfortable with your research or don't have time, ask a compliance consultant or experienced attorney for input.

The next thing to do is to make sure you have a written policy and procedure for handling a breach. This needs to be consistent with the applicable laws and any Business Associate Agreements you have in place. You might assume procedures and timelines for breach notifications are standard documents, but they are not. If, for instance, your BAA says that the subcontractor has to notify the Business Associate within five business days of discovering a breach, then you need to make sure your policy includes language outlining breach notification timelines ("no later than five business days after discovering the breach"). Also make sure you include the right people as you draft this policy and procedure; include anyone who would be affected by the procedures or who should have oversight. Also include a step, as a reminder, to identify the various state laws that the breach implicates. This comes into play when the patients live in different states—you need to review those laws or have legal counsel assist, because state laws differ and may have different reporting or notification requirements. And if your patients are international-check the European Union's General Data Protection Regulation (GDPR) requirements.

Next, put together specific procedures for the risk assessment. Be sure your process helps you get all the information you need for the notification and evaluation, such as the following:

- What data elements were exposed?
- How many patients' data were compromised?
- Where, when, and how did the breach occur?
- Who was responsible for the breach? (an employee, sub-contractor, system problem, etc.)
- Did the information leave the organization? (internal snooping versus a file sent to the wrong entity)
- Were you able to mitigate the risk? (for example, by retrieving the records)

Depending on the outcome of this breach risk assessment, you will likely have to notify the individual or individuals who were the subjects of the information and the Department of Health and Human Services. If you are a Business Associate, your first duty is to notify the Covered Entity whose data was compromised. If you are a subcontractor to a Business Associate, you have an obligation to notify of a breach. In that instance, you would call the party who is a Business Associate to determine how to proceed, unless you have an agreement that states otherwise.

If, after you conduct your risk assessment, you find that there were many individuals affected or the breach was more than a simple one-time error, it's a very good idea to touch base with an attorney or consultant with expertise in this area, even if only to double-check your approach. Handling a breach can be overwhelming when you haven't done it before, so it's worth the small investment to get help; the experience and learning will be useful if there is ever another breach event.

Last, keep in mind that in addition to HIPAA and the state-level breach notification laws, there is also the FTC's Health Breach Notification Rule, which is covered in Chapter 5, "Federal Trade Commission." If you are covered under HIPAA, the FTC Health Breach Notification Rule won't matter to you, but if you are a developer or other non–Covered Entity, you should be aware of this rule, especially because the FTC enforces it. Regardless of which rule applies to you, the steps above will serve you well as you build your processes. Lastly, if you are handling international patient's information, the European Union's GDPR provides strict protections, beyond the scope of this book, but be aware, especially if you are designing solutions intended for this broad use.

Conclusion

The HIPAA rules, along with the related state and federal laws, are foundational for health tech developers and providers who rely on technology in their practices (which is virtually all practitioners, in one way or another).

If you haven't dealt with these rules in the past, starting from scratch can be daunting. Similarly, if you develop healthcare technology but haven't been involved with healthcare compliance or regulations, you may not easily understand the nexus between the rules and the operational reality. If this describes you, you can save yourself many headaches and potential mistakes by bringing onboard someone with that type of expertise to help focus and guide this aspect of your practice's or company's development.

The other important point is to remember that the HIPAA Security Rule is scalable, so not all elements are required for all entities, but you do need to evaluate them in light of your own organization and risks.

If you choose to outsource your IT functions, and you are a Covered Entity under HIPAA, do not assume that hiring an IT company means you've met the requirements. Most IT vendors, for instance, do not assume the responsibilities of the designated security official. Be very sure you understand what you need to do and who is doing it. Many IT vendors are great at developing software or setting up systems, but they may not be regulatory experts. Have this important discussion with potential vendors so you know what gaps you need to address internally. You do *not* want to have a breach and then find out that you didn't have a privacy or security officer designated (which is required under the HIPAA rules). I don't mean to beat a dead horse, but I've seen this happen repeatedly; it's a very common misunderstanding and one that can be costly.

CHAPTER 3

Health and Human Services: Office of the National Coordinator for Health Information Technology and Other Agencies

Who Needs to Read This: Healthcare providers, health information exchanges (HIEs), health information networks (HINs), and health IT developers.

Office of the National Coordinator for Health Information Technology

The Office of the National Coordinator for Health Information Technology (ONC), an agency situated within Health and Human Services, is the primary federal entity responsible for coordinating nationwide efforts to promote advanced healthcare information technology and the electronic exchange of health information. ONC was created in 2004 through an Executive Order and was legislatively mandated in the Health Information Technology for Economic and Clinical Health Act (HITECH Act) of 2009.[29]

Although ONC is intimately involved with many aspects of healthcare technology, we're focusing here on the Cures Act, specifically the anti-information-blocking requirements applicable to both developers and providers and the related Final Rules.

The 21st Century Cures Act

The 21st Century Cures Act: Interoperability, Information Blocking, and the ONC Health IT Certification Program, also known as the Cures Act, includes many provisions related to streamlining the development of drugs and devices as well as enhancing health information interoperability and removing barriers to information sharing.[30] This act affects healthcare providers, health tech vendors, health information exchanges, and health information networks. The Cures Act has largely flown under the radar for many but is significant in its requirements and in the broad range of entities it affects.

The ONC released the following general statement about the purpose of the Cures Act:

> The seamless exchange of electronic health information and patient use of smartphone applications (apps) hold huge potential for delivering affordability and quality through transparency and competition. In 2016, Congress passed the 21st Century Cures Act to drive the electronic access, exchange, and use of health information. The Office of the National Coordinator for Health Information Technology (ONC) Cures Act Final Rule implements the interoperability provisions of the Cures Act to promote patient control over their own health information.
>
> For the American public, the Cures Act Final Rule fosters innovation in health care to deliver better information, more conveniently, to patients and their providers. It also promotes transparency through modern technology, providing tremendous opportunities for the American public to gain visibility into the services, quality, and costs of health care. As ONC implements the Cures Act Final Rule's requirements, patients will begin to get on-demand access to certain information within their medical records, specifically the United States Core Data for Interoperability, which includes clinical notes, test results, and medications. Over the next two years, patients will be increasingly able to choose apps to assemble and read their records, allowing them to shop for care by comparing costs, understanding possible treatments, and expected health outcomes.

The Cures Act Final Rule includes provisions that require support for modern computing standards and APIs (application programming interfaces). These technical provisions will inject competition into health care by promoting an entrepreneurial economy and new business models using smartphone apps to provide novel services and new choices in care. The Cures Act Final Rule will also make sure health information follows a patient by preventing industrywide information blocking practices and other anti-competitive behavior by those entrusted to hold patients' electronic health information.[31]

Anti-information-blocking, in a nutshell, requires that patients have complete and immediate access to their electronic medical records, free of charge. Only a couple types of records are excluded: those created in anticipation of litigation and psychotherapy notes.

For our purposes, the anti-information-blocking section of the Cures Act is intended to enhance access to patient health information. Individuals and entities that are allowed access to health data under HIPAA cannot be prevented from or delayed in accessing that data. Providers need to make sure patients can access their data, and developers need to understand this requirement as part of the front-end development process.

Note: The 21st Century Cures Act does not mandate the creation of a patient portal. This is often misunderstood, and the portal is now a reality for many healthcare organizations, but it's *not* required under the Cures Act.

Information Blocking

What is *information blocking*? According to the ONC:

"Information blocking is a practice by an "actor" that is likely to interfere with the access, exchange, or use of electronic health information (EHI), except as required by law or specified in an information blocking exception. The Cures Act applied the law to healthcare providers, health IT developers of certified health IT, and health information exchanges (HIEs)/health information networks (HINs).

It is also important to note that the Cures Act established two different "knowledge" standards for actors' practices within the statute's definition of "information blocking." In particular, for health IT developers of certified health IT, as well as HIEs/HINs, the law applies the standard of whether they know, or should know, that a practice is likely to interfere with the access, exchange, or use of EHI. For healthcare providers, the law applies the standard of whether they know that the practice is unreasonable and is likely to interfere with the access, exchange, or use of EHI.[32]"

Let's be more specific about who is affected by the Cures Act provisions we're discussing in this chapter:

- *Healthcare providers* (not necessarily Covered Entities under HIPAA).
- *Health information exchanges (HIEs) and health information networks (HINs).* These are any entities that facilitate data exchange between providers, including Business Associates performing this function.
- *Health IT (HIT) developers.* These provide or offer certified electronic health record technology.

Information Blocking for Providers

For providers, anti-information-blocking means that patient records must be completed in a timely manner and made available, regardless of the actual request process. If you are a healthcare provider, are you getting your records completed, signed, and entered into the system punctually?

The law requires records be made available "immediately" but doesn't define that time frame. As a provider, you will want to define that standard in your internal policies and make sure everyone affected is educated to that requirement and is following it. That's the front end and is less about technology and more about getting your records-completion process tightened up. Records need to be reviewed and signed in order to be made available. Education for both your providers and your medical records team is important here.

On the back end, anti-information-blocking means having a process (often, but not required to be, a portal) that enables patients to access their records. Whether it's a portal or a more manual record-request process, it's important for providers to review their process with the responsible staff and identify any areas where delays can occur. For instance, if you're not using a portal and it is one person's job to review requests, what happens when that person is out sick or on vacation? Is there a fail-safe backup? You should walk through the record-request process, from request to fulfillment, and review each step to make sure it's as efficient as possible. Address any potential glitches along the way.

Organizations setting up a patient portal have other matters to consider: How will you handle the medical records of minors? It's easy to say that parents are allowed access, but state laws come into play here. Treatment related to reproduction, substance abuse, and mental health is commonly subject to different consent requirements, state by state, for minors.

Which records must be included on a portal? Although this is answered in the final rule, a provider may be reluctant to post lab test results, for instance, without first discussing them with the patient. Because these requirements are still relatively new, and don't have any enforcement history, it's not surprising that some providers evaluate the potential harm to the patient versus 100 percent compliance.

For instance, applicable state law says a 16-year-old girl is allowed to consent to healthcare services related to a pregnancy without telling her parents. The practitioner knows that the patient lives in an abusive situation (parental) and the parents' knowledge of the daughter's pregnancy and plan to get an abortion would escalate an already tenuous domestic situation. The daughter is on the parent's insurance, but wants to pay cash and keep the records from her parents. How can she do that? Who can have access to her records? This is the type of question to consider (a team approach is good here—experts in the system's technical design, medical records personnel, and even clinical staff will all have valuable perspectives).

These sorts of ethical and legal dilemmas are not new; HIPAA created many of them with institution of patient rights and various regulatory standards, which were often confusing when lined up against state laws on consent. To some, this is purely an exercise in legal applicability. To others, these represent serious moral issues that are, or should be, in a discretionary gray area, where the likelihood of harm is considered.

One key point to understand regarding which records need to be made available: This applies to electronic medical records. The law does not require providers to go through all their historical paper records and upload them so they are available through a portal. Note, however, that the HIPAA right to access still applies, so this is really just a process matter.

Keep in mind that HIPAA allows up to 30 days to respond to a medical record request; the Cures Act doesn't define the timeframe but is clear that records must be available to patients without delay. Providers commonly interpret this as 24 to 48 hours, depending on the provider and type of records. If you have a portal, that turnaround is feasible. It's not clear how the discrepancy in timeframes will be addressed.

Information Blocking for Exchanges, Networks, and Developers

For HIEs, HINs, and HIT developers, anti-information-blocking means that the tools you develop, provide, and use need to be built with consideration of how access is managed. Are redundancies or unnecessary roadblocks being built in? Are there any barriers to data exchange? The tools themselves need to facilitate smooth access and data exchange, while also addressing the necessary safeguards required under the HIPAA Security Rule.

Of course, the tools are only as good as the humans using them. To the extent providers or others are needed to take action, for instance, to grant access, those users need to be thoroughly trained, and systems or processes should be in place to ensure that the accountable individuals are notified. Once the tool is properly developed and the processes established, it's up to the providers and other users to use them appropriately to avoid causing delays.

Exceptions to Anti-Information-Blocking Provisions

There are exceptions to the Cures Act anti-information-blocking provisions, most of which are intuitive and practical.

- **Denial Exception:** Access may be denied if preventing access will protect the patient or others from harm. As you would expect, there needs to be solid documentation supporting the decision to deny access. The justification needs to include the basis, or reasonable belief, that denying access would prevent or reduce harm. Also, the access denial needs to be narrowly tailored to apply to only that information that could be harmful. Obviously, this exception would be based on human judgment, most likely the provider's, and applies either when the provider, in his or her professional judgment, believes the information would be harmful or when the data is known to be inaccurate or corrupted in some way that would render it damaging.

- **Privacy Exception:** This exception relates specifically to state and federal privacy law requirements. For instance, a provider would choose not to release data if that release first required a patient authorization by law or if the patient had put legally allowed restrictions on the disclosure. The provider would not be violating the Cures Act if they adhere to applicable privacy laws. It's always important to make sure that any such denials are documented along with the reason. Communication about the reason for the denial, in accordance with HIPAA or the applicable state law, is expected.

- **Security Exception:** This exception, as you might expect, applies to those denials that are made in the interest of data security. The key here is to make sure the denial is specific to the security threat and is not overly broad or applied in any discriminatory fashion. To use this exception, the organization needs to have appropriate privacy and security policies in place that are consistent with the denial.

- **Infeasibility Exception:** This exception, too, is just like it sounds. If it is not feasible to allow access, the organization may deny the request. This applies in several types of circumstances:

- Uncontrollable events—things like natural disasters, public health emergencies, labor unrest or strikes, telecommunications or internet interruptions, or some regulatory action are examples. The Final Rule clarifies that the event must actually make the action infeasible. The simple existence of a hurricane, for instance, is not sufficient unless the storm created widespread power outages and related problems that resulted in an organization's inability to perform the necessary functions properly.

- Segmentation—this one is not so intuitive, at least not to a nontechnical person. Segmentation applies when the "organization cannot fulfill the request for access, exchange, or use of EHI because it cannot unambiguously segment the requested EHI."
- Infeasibility under the circumstances—this is when the organization can demonstrate through the use of a contemporaneous record or other documentation that the request cannot be satisfied under the circumstances. This exception is rather broad and general, but it's important, again, to note that this needs to be well-reasoned and documented.
- The use of the Infeasibility Exception requires that the organization denying the request provide a response within 10 days that includes the reason for the denial.
- **Health IT Performance Exception:** This exception applies when issues like maintenance or system downtime make it impossible for the organization to fulfill a request. In this instance, the performance practice must
    - Be for a period of time no longer than necessary to conduct the maintenance, repair, and so forth
    - Be implemented in a consistent and nondiscriminatory fashion
    - Meet certain requirements if the unavailability is initiated by a health IT developer of certified health IT, a HIE, or a HIN
- In some instances, the health tech company and the provider may be at odds when the performance of a health tech app impacts the provider's ability to meet regulatory requirements. It's important for developers and other health tech companies to understand the requirements and to

ensure that downtime or other interruptions are kept to the minimum time possible, are in no way inconsistent or discriminatory, and are in alignment with the service-level agreements, statements of work, or whatever contractual arrangements are applicable.

- **Content and Manner Exception:** In general, organizations must fulfill a request for access in any manner requested except to the extent they are technically unable to do so or when they cannot come to an agreement with the requestor about the terms or manner of the request. The request must be for information covered by the final rule, and the request must be for access in a manner that is feasible and agreed on.

- **Fees Exception:** This exception allows organizations that fulfill requests to charge fees related to the costs of technology development and interoperability. It's important to note, however, that the organization still needs to apply fees in a nondiscriminatory fashion and in accordance with both HIPAA and applicable state laws, which often set the allowable rates.

- **Licensing Exception:** This exception allows organizations to protect their own innovations, including by charging fees as a return on their investment in development. In other words, health tech developers can charge licensing fees without it being considered an information-blocking activity or violation of this Cures Act rule.

- TEFCA Manner Exception: This final exception was added to the final rule and is applicable when an actor will only fulfill requests for access, use, or exchange of EHI by way of the Trusted Exchange Framework and Common Agreement (TEFCA). To satisfy this TEFCA Manner Exception, both the actor and requestor must be part of TEFCA as well as meet other specifications.

On December 13, 2023, ONC published another final rule: "Health Data, Technology, and Interoperability: Certification Program Updates,

Algorithm Transparency, and Information Sharing," known as HTI-1 Final Rule, which implements the Electronic Health Record Reporting requirement under the Cures Act in the *Federal Register*. This Final Rule revises the current Health IT Certification Program and formalizes and updates certain Cures Act requirements related to health IT. It also provides some clarification that is useful in the discussion of the anti-information-blocking rule. Developers should review the requirements for certification.

One noteworthy aspect of the HTI-1 Final Rule is the definition of what it means to "offer health IT":

> "To hold out for sale, resale, license, or relicense; or to sell, resell, license, relicense, or otherwise provide or supply [ONC-certified health IT] for deployment by or for other individual(s) or entity(ies) under any arrangement [except as provided below]."

Why is this significant? It could be impactful in a situation where a nondeveloper, such as a large health system, develops and shares its health IT systems and processes, for instance, with physicians in the community. As noted above, there are exclusions, such as when the provision of health IT is purely through funding and not actual sharing of a system. Activities involving purely performing services involving healthcare IT, as well as consulting and legal services, would not be included.

To-Do List

Providers: If you aren't already aware of the above requirements related to patients' access to their medical records, review your existing policies and procedures and evaluate any patient portal or other electronic processes for record exchange.

- Which records are included in the record set available to patients?
- How quickly are records uploaded, including labs, X-rays, and procedure reports?
- Do you maintain records in non-electronic format? If so, look over processes for those as well.

Although the Cures Act doesn't require you to upload all past paper records into a patient portal, you are still required to provide those paper records to patients under HIPAA. This is a good time to take a look at all your processes for record requests, keeping in mind that the goal of all these regulations is to give patients access to, and control over, their health information.

Developers: You need to be well-versed in many requirements under the Cures Act. In creating this book, I've focused on the laws applicable to healthcare technology, but not the specific requirements for issues such as certification. That being said, some key suggestions include the following:

- Do a deep dive into the ONC site (healthit.gov) and the various regulations and guidance generated by that agency. It is on point for the federal government's oversight of interoperability and transparency of healthcare technology.
- Evaluate your current checklists for development. Are you addressing all the regulatory requirements?
- Bookmark the ONC website as well as others suggested in this book that may be relevant to your product or services.

Other HHS Agency Rules and Guidance
Agency for Healthcare Research and Quality

The Agency for Healthcare Research and Quality (AHRQ), an HHS agency, has issued pertinent guidance for developers of digital healthcare: *Evidence- and Consensus-Based Digital Healthcare Equity Framework*. This document, published in February 2024, "guides users in intentionally considering equity in healthcare solutions that involve digital technologies."[33] The document also features an implementation guide that I recommend for developers. This framework is useful in that it discusses the topic of equity during the technology development phase and utilization of such technologies.

According to AHRQ, the framework is structured around the digital healthcare life cycle and is aligned with commonly used quality improvement approaches. The guidance is centered around the following stages:

- Planning
- Development
- Acquisition
- Implementation/Maintenance
- Monitoring/Improvement/Equity
- Assessment of healthcare solutions that involve digital technologies

Another key aspect of this guidance is the specific recommended inclusion of various stakeholder groups in the development/framework process, including (a) digital healthcare developers and vendors; (b) health systems; (c) health plans; (d) clinical providers; (e) patients/caregivers, patient advocates, and community champions; (f) policymakers; and (g) public entities. This is a valuable reminder to develop products and the resulting procedures with the appropriate involvement of affected stakeholders.

It's very easy to get a workgroup together and get a project going, but success is more likely when you evaluate all your users, patients, and others impacted and solicit their engagement. This is particularly relevant for organizations working toward increased automation, use of AI, and value-based care models. It's important to be mindful of the end goal of improving patient care, efficiency, and cost outcomes and not to become completely engrossed in the technical aspects so that the human and business needs are secondary concerns.

In addition, this framework outlines six different guiding principles that differ a great deal from the other documents in this book. These principles are focused on patients and outcomes rather than rules and process. From the *Evidence- and Consensus-Based Digital Healthcare Equity Framework*, the principles are as follows:

Guiding Principle 1: Ensure digital healthcare solutions that involve digital technologies ameliorate, not exacerbate, inequities. Digital healthcare technologies should be utilized to address health inequities and to close any gaps in the quality of care. To ensure that digital healthcare solutions do not exacerbate inequities and to avoid worsening any existing disparities, different strategies should be considered across the lifecycle of digital health-care solutions.

Guiding Principle 2: Represent equity through person-centeredness. Digital healthcare equity needs to be achieved through a person-centered approach, which considers the needs of the patient and caregiver, provider, and healthcare system in different settings and throughout the digital healthcare lifecycle.

Guiding Principle 3: Encourage inclusivity and participatory creation of digital healthcare solutions. The inclusive and participatory creation of healthcare solutions that involve digital technologies can be achieved through the co-creation and engagement of diverse groups and representatives of different stakeholders' subpopulations such as patients, users, providers, and vendors. An example would be training digital healthcare developers and vendors to work with different populations to assess and address health equity literacy among digital healthcare developers and vendors. It also requires strategic and organizational focus on patient and community engagement throughout the digital healthcare lifecycle. Moreover, user experiences should be a guiding principle to ensure healthcare solutions that involve digital technologies properly address all users' needs and desires.

Guiding Principle 4: Supporting effective implementation in diverse settings. Achieving digital healthcare equity requires considerations of the different settings in which digital healthcare solutions are implemented. Being mindful of the context of implementation ensures that the tailoring of digital healthcare solutions will be accessible by diverse groups.

Guiding Principle 5: Ensure specific attention to policy/regulatory relevance or impact of the proposed solutions. Achieving digital healthcare equity requires special attention to the influence of regulatory and legislative actions on improving patient health. Relevant policy/regulatory efforts can ensure equity intentionality across the digital healthcare lifecycle. An example of such policies would be that sexual orientation and gender identity be documented in electronic health records. This policy impacted the collection of sexual orientation and gender identity data across different patient populations. Moreover, different policies and regulatory constraints, such as those related to interoperability or confidentiality of data may impose benefits and harms for digital healthcare solutions and present the impact of policy and regulatory factors on achieving digital healthcare equity.

Guiding Principle 6: Focus on impact and outcomes for patients, health systems, and communities. The digital healthcare equity framework should focus on paths for impacting care delivery and health outcomes and help stakeholders achieve equitable health outcomes for different patient populations. </EXT>

So, what does all this mean? Think of this less as a legal standard and more as a plan that enables you to incorporate patient-centered aspects into technology solutions in the development stage and beyond. Also keep in mind the continuous movement toward patient access to records, cybersecurity (which is ultimately a patient care issue, too), and better reimbursement and care methodologies, such as value-based care.

All of these issues are geared toward providing a better healthcare experience for the patient and, hopefully, a reduction in costs. With AI, one concern has been ensuring that the data AI systems rely on is not biased or discriminatory. The framework and principles are another attempt at providing us with a checklist of considerations as we design, build, and implement new solutions or enhance old ones.

The Centers for Medicare & Medicaid Services (CMS) and the Office of Civil Rights (OCR)

CMS and the OCR have partnered to update the Affordable Care Act (ACA) Section 1557 with a new final rule that includes requirements for nondiscrimination in the use of AI in healthcare. This rule, like the guidance issued by the US Patent and Trademark Office, was spurred by President Biden's Executive Order on Safe, Secure, and Trustworthy Development and Use of Artificial Intelligence.[34]

The updated final rule was published on April 24, 2024, under 45 C.F.R. § 92.210. If you are familiar with Section 1557, you may recall it is a nondiscrimination in healthcare rule that applies to recipients of federal financial assistance, HHS, and entities established under Title I of the ACA, including state exchanges and federally facilitated exchanges (collectively, Covered Entities) to prevent them from discriminating on the basis of race, color, national origin, sex, age, or disability in health programs or activities through the use of "patient care decision support tools." A *patient care decision support tool*, which is a newly defined term that replaces *clinical algorithm* in the rule, is "any automated or non-automated tool, mechanism, method, technology, or combination thereof used by a Covered Entity to support clinical decision-making in its health programs or activities."

Conclusion

The *Evidence- and Consensus-Based Digital Healthcare Equity Framework* does not have any regulatory teeth but is a good document to review as you put together the structure for evaluating your development process, stakeholders, and impacts on end users. Issues such as patient socioeconomic status, demographics, and other nontechnical factors should be baked in to your processes to facilitate (hopefully) the best possible outcomes for providers and patients who will use the digital health technologies you've developed.

CHAPTER 4

Food and Drug Administration

Who Needs to Read This: Anyone developing a medical device, including Software as a Medical Device; anyone purchasing such medical devices for their practices.

The Food and Drug Administration may not be the first agency you think of when contemplating the regulatory requirements applicable to health tech devices, services, and applications. By its very name, the agency is responsible for the safety of food and drug products. The Federal Food, Drug, and Cosmetic Act (FDCA) is one of the core laws the FDA oversees and enforces.

But the FDA has evolved as technology has advanced. The FDA now has purview over two aspects related to health technology compliance: the regulation of medical devices and the cybersecurity of those devices. It's important to remember, too, that AI and machine learning (ML) software are often categorized as medical devices, so the FDA will become a more visible player in the regulation of healthcare technology as AI becomes a bigger and bigger component of healthcare developments.

The Federal Food, Drug, and Cosmetic Act and Regulated Medical Devices

The Federal Food, Drug, and Cosmetic Act is the applicable US law in the regulation of medical devices.

When considering the applicability to medical devices of FDA requirements, the first determination you must make is whether your product constitutes a "medical device." And keep in mind, some software can be categorized as a medical device (Software as a Medical Device, or SaMD). This is the route by which the FDA will have leverage over AI.

The Center for Devices and Radiological Health (CDRH) is the division of the FDA that regulates medical devices. Its role is to evaluate the safety and effectiveness of medical devices, both before and after they've gone to market. This authority dates back to a 1976 amendment to the Food, Drug, and Cosmetics Act and other subsequent laws. Section 201(h) of the FDCA defines a *medical device* as follows:

- Instrument, apparatus, machine, implant, in vitro reagent, including component, part, or accessory
- Diagnoses, cures, mitigates, treats, or prevents disease or condition
- Affects structure or function of body
- Doesn't achieve purpose as a drug
- Excludes *certain* software functions (data storage, administrative support, electronic patient records)

This definition is obviously broad and encompasses many wearable and implantable devices as well as software. Software as a Medical Device, or SaMD, has been defined by the International Medical Device Regulators Forum (IMDRF) as "SaMD intended to be used for one or more medical purposes that perform these purposes without being part of a hardware medical device." A *medical purpose* under the Food, Drug, and Cosmetic Act is a purpose "intended to treat, diagnose, care, mitigate, or prevent disease or other conditions." That definition, too, is very broad, and with the proliferation of AI/ML software, the FDA is continuing to refine how those specific technologies are evaluated, especially given the ongoing changes and evolution of adaptive software.

What about the generative AI tools that we hear about on the news every day? The large language models (LLMs) are AI that is trained on very large datasets, which enables them to recognize, summarize, translate, predict, and generate content (for example: ChatGPT, Llama, Claude, and PaLM). Although there is much interest and development happening that incorporate the LLM model, the FDA did note in its October 2023 update that no device has been authorized that uses generative AI or artificial general intelligence (AGI) or that is powered by large language models.[35]

The FDA explains how it views the regulation of AI and ML medical devices as follows:

> "Traditionally, the FDA reviews medical devices through an appropriate premarket pathway, such as premarket clearance (510(k)), De Novo classification, or premarket approval. The FDA may also review and clear modifications to medical devices, including software as a medical device, depending on the significance or risk posed to patients of that modification. . . .
>
> The FDA's traditional paradigm of medical device regulation was not designed for adaptive artificial intelligence and machine learning technologies. Under the FDA's current approach to software modifications, the FDA anticipates that many of these artificial intelligence and machine learning–driven software changes to a device may need a premarket review.
>
> On April 2, 2019, the FDA published a discussion paper "Proposed Regulatory Framework for Modifications to Artificial Intelligence/Machine Learning (AI/ML)-Based Software as a Medical Device (SaMD)—Discussion Paper and Request for Feedback," that describes the FDA's foundation for a potential approach to premarket review for artificial intelligence and machine learning–driven software modifications.
>
> The ideas described in the discussion paper leverage practices from our current premarket programs and rely on IMDRF's risk categorization principles, the FDA's benefit-risk framework, risk management principles described in the software modifications guidance, and the organization-based total product lifecycle approach (also envisioned in the Digital Health Software Precertification (Pre-Cert) Program).

In the framework described in the discussion paper, the FDA envisions a "predetermined change control plan" in premarket submissions. This plan would include the types of anticipated modifications—referred to as the "Software as a Medical Device Pre-Specifications"—and the associated methodology being used to implement those changes in a controlled manner that manages risks to patients—referred to as the "Algorithm Change Protocol."

In this potential approach, the FDA would expect a commitment from manufacturers on transparency and real-world performance monitoring for artificial intelligence and machine learning–based software as a medical device, as well as periodic updates to the FDA on what changes were implemented as part of the approved pre-specifications and the algorithm change protocol.

Such a regulatory framework could enable the FDA and manufacturers to evaluate and monitor a software product from its premarket development to postmarket performance. This approach could allow for the FDA's regulatory oversight to embrace the iterative improvement power of artificial intelligence and machine learning–based software as a medical device, while assuring patient safety.

As part of the AI/ML Action Plan, the FDA is highlighting its intention to develop an update to the proposed regulatory framework presented in the AI/ML-based SaMD discussion paper, including through the issuance of a draft guidance on the predetermined change control plan.[36]"

This summary from the FDA references several valuable resources that I would advise anyone in this space to become familiar with.

One more interesting piece of data from the FDA is the types of "devices" that are in, or have been through, the approval process: 87 percent of devices on this list authorized in calendar year 2022 are in radiology (122), followed by 7 percent in cardiovascular (10), and 1 percent each in neurology (2), hematology (1), gastroenterology/urology (1), ophthalmic (2), clinical chemistry (1), and ear, nose, and throat (1).

You can find a treasure trove of information on the FDA website, including all the publicly available information about the specific devices.

If you're interested in this area, take a little time to check out that website.

If you've ever reviewed the FDA's approval process, you know that the FDA has a complex set of requirements pertaining to medical devices, depending on how they are classified. Anyone seeking to develop a non-software medical device or who is unsure whether their product could be classified as a medical device will want to familiarize themselves with the voluminous medical device requirements. Note that some requirements are "premarket," so you must have a solid understanding on the front end of your development process. The FDA advises developers and manufacturers to look at intended use and indications for use of their product to make that determination.

Also, *combination products* are covered by the FDA. These are products that include a combination of drug, device, and/or biologic, for example, drug-eluting stents. The FDA exercises jurisdiction over combination products, but which "arm" of the FDA depends on the components.

The degree of regulatory control is contingent on the device classification, I, II, or III. Classification is based on the description and intended use of the product. The higher the number, the greater the degree of risk. You can find the actual regulations at 21 C.F.R. Parts 801–820.[37] These regulations outline specific controls that may apply to different classifications of devices. Once you establish the appropriate category for your device, review the regulatory controls that apply. They include a range of requirements such as for design, testing, and labeling. This is all important information to have at the start of product development.

As you can see, getting a product to market requires a number of steps. The FDA provides a lot of guidance on its website, but if you aren't experienced at handling the FDA requirements and process, you need to have a trusted resource to assist you. The specific process steps, which are currently evolving, are also very detailed and vary by product, so are beyond the scope of this book. By the time this book is in your hands, a whole new set of guidance or regulations will probably be in process, particularly with respect to SaMD.

In addition to the FDA, the International Medical Device Regulators Forum provides extensive resources not only for the recommended processes (developed in conjunction with the FDA) but also for cybersecurity. I recommend reviewing and bookmarking the IMDRF website if this subject matter pertains to you: www.imdrf.org.[38] This organization has working groups that address artificial intelligence, personalized medical devices, and Software as a Medical Device. Each group has published a variety of documents and resources. It's definitely worth checking out if you are working on a device that will need regulatory approval.

Cybersecurity

In a recent publication, *Best Practices for Communicating Cybersecurity Vulnerabilities to Patients*, the Center for Devices and Radiological Health (a division of the FDA) outlines its role as follows:

> "The U.S. Food and Drug Administration's (FDA's) Center for Devices and Radiological Health (CDRH) remains committed to its mission to promote and protect the public health, including the safe and effective use of medical devices that are connected to the internet, hospital networks, and other medical devices (hereafter referred to as "connected medical devices"). These medical devices range from software as a medical device (SaMD) such as phone applications, to implantable medical devices, such as pacemakers. The increased use of connected medical devices in the United States has led to an increase in cybersecurity vulnerabilities. The FDA is at the forefront of helping mitigate cybersecurity issues related to the use of connected medical devices. Currently, the FDA's safety communications fall into two main categories: device-specific information, and software and hardware supply-chain issues.[39]"

As you can see, the FDA is very engaged in security as it relates to the various healthcare devices we are discussing here. Much of the emphasis from the FDA, however, relates to education and communication rather than enforcement. The FDA stresses the importance of communication about security risks and the safeguards to take for patients and caregivers. Clear communication, which includes a discussion of risks and benefits, is of huge importance, according to the FDA.

Also important is the availability of the information to consumers and users. In one section of the guidance, the FDA states the following:

"Safety communications on cybersecurity risks are more easily found if they incorporate best practices in search engine optimization (SEO) techniques, such as:

- including the name of the manufacturer and device name (or device category name) in the title of the communication, if the cybersecurity vulnerability is specific to a medical device or group of medical devices;
- including other important keywords that patients may search for near the beginning of the title, such as the name of the cybersecurity vulnerability; and
- incorporating important keywords in the content itself, including the list of specific medical devices, as well as the associated diseases or conditions.[40]"

The FDA's Digital Health Center of Excellence is another resource that can be found through the FDA website. It states the following:

"The Digital Health Center of Excellence empowers digital health stakeholders to advance health care by fostering responsible and high-quality digital health innovation. We provide services in the following functional areas for digital health:
- Regulatory Innovation
- Strategic Partnerships
- Digital Health Policy and Technology Support and Training
- Medical Device Cybersecurity
- Artificial Intelligence / Machine Learning
- Regulatory Science Advancement
- Regulatory Review Support and Coordination
- Advanced Manufacturing
- Real World
- Evidence and Advanced Clinical Studies [41]"

According to its own fact sheet, the FDA works with various federal agencies, including the Department of Homeland Security, and device manufacturers, healthcare organizations, security experts and researchers, and end users to enhance the security of US critical cyber infrastructure.

I recommend that anyone planning to develop a health tech device or app reviews the FDA cybersecurity resources. Although these don't have the weight of regulatory requirement, it's always a good idea to adhere to government guidance and certainly to take advantage of available tools and guidance.

Conclusion

As you can see, the FDA is a very active player in the regulation of medical devices, including those that incorporate any AI elements.

If you are contemplating developing a device or SaMD, I strongly encourage you to spend some time on the FDA site to understand where your device or product likely fits, what approvals are needed, and any key standards you must meet.

Also, as I often advise, find an expert in this arena to help guide you through the process. There are many nuances, and with the technology advancements, the FDA is also updating its own practices, so having a trusted advisor is a solid and recommended investment.

CHAPTER 5

Federal Trade Commission

Who Needs to Read This: Healthcare technology companies that use personal health data in their products or services; healthcare company marketing departments.

In general, the Federal Trade Commission is tasked with consumer protection, which includes overseeing communication about products and services to ensure that representations about efficacy and safety are accurate and not misleading to the public. You won't find healthcare or technology listed as an industry the FTC regulates. But if you look at the FTC website and click on Advice and Guidance, Privacy and Security, there they are: Health Privacy, Consumer Privacy, Data Security, Red Flag Rules (which reside under the Fair Credit Reporting Act), and Tech.[42]

The FTC has very broad authority: The commission may "prosecute any inquiry necessary to its duties in any part of the United States" (FTC Act Sec. 3, 15 U.S.C. Sec. 43) and is authorized "to gather and compile information concerning, and to investigate from time to time the organization, business, conduct, practices, and management of any person, partnership, or corporation engaged in or whose business affects commerce, excepting banks, savings and loan institutions . . . Federal credit unions . . . and common carriers" (FTC Act Sec. 6[a], 15 U.S.C. Sec. 46[a]).[43]

The good news is that most of what you find on the FTC site is, indeed, not enforcement-related laws, rules, or regulations, but there is a large volume of useful guidance. The FTC is very interested in data security and technology. The bad news (if you happen to be on the wrong side of the issues) is that the FTC is getting into the business of enforcing its existing rules, and it has been very transparent in its warnings. You will find the FTC enforcing the Health Breach Notification Rule, the Federal Trade Commission Act (FTCA) (which relates to unfair and deceptive trade practices), and the Children's Online Privacy Protection Act (COPPA), as well as antitrust laws.

The Health Breach Notification Rule

The FTC's Health Breach Notification Rule applies to what we're discussing here. The final rule was issued on August 24, 2009 (16 C.F.R. Part 318), as required under the American Recovery and Reinvestment Act of 2009, with a compliance date of February 22, 2010. The FTC updated the rule on April 26, 2024, primarily to include clarification previously contained in its 2021 memo, discussed below.

The Health Breach Notification Rule covers vendors of personal health records (PHRs) that contain individually identifiable health information "created or received by health care providers" as well as entities that offer products and services through online services of vendors of personal health records, including mobile apps. More specifically, *PHRs* are defined as electronic records of "identifiable health information on an individual that has the technical capacity to draw information from multiple sources and that is managed, shared, and controlled by or primarily for the individual" (from 16 C.F.R. Part 318).

So, what does that mean? It means that this rule applies to not only vendors of personal health records, PHR-related entities, and their service providers but also companies that collect or store medical records on behalf of individuals and companies that provide apps that help consumers manage a health condition or health-related activities by collecting their health data. Service providers, such as data hosting providers, are also included. This does *not* include HIPAA Covered Entities or Business Associates, but note that the FTC and HIPAA breach reporting requirements are very similar. The rationale behind this was to ensure that consumers receive only one breach notification, preferably from the entity with which the consumer is familiar (rather than an unknown vendor, for instance). The *Federal Register* outlines scenarios to guide entities covered under both rules about how best to provide consumer notification.

Prior to this rule (and subsequent clarification), many apps in the marketplace were largely unregulated with respect to the privacy and security of healthcare data. Healthcare-related apps that were regulated were covered under HIPAA (what I referred to earlier as "provider apps"). As a result, only apps that were directly related to providing healthcare services (such as those connected to a provider's office) or billing for healthcare services or for their Business Associates were required to implement specific controls and notifications. All the rest were not. The FTC, the agency responsible for consumer protection, wasn't really on the radar in terms of regulatory oversight in this arena. But it is now.

The Health Breach Notification Rule went largely unnoticed or, perhaps, was misunderstood until the commission issued a policy statement, *Statement of the Commission on Breaches by Health Apps and Other Connected Devices*, on September 15, 2021, in which the FTC clarified key components of the rule, "in recognition of the proliferation of apps and connected devices that capture sensitive health data."

According to the policy statement, the Health Breach Notification Rule "helps to ensure that entities who are not covered by the Health Insurance Portability and Accountability Act ('HIPAA') nevertheless face accountability when consumers' sensitive health information is compromised." The Health Breach Notification Rule is not new, but this clarification, which has now been largely incorporated into the updated rule, is and signals enforcement of a rule that has mostly gone unenforced to date. The push to regulate apps came from Congress, and further legislation is likely.

One part of the rule that might be misunderstood is who the FTC considers a "health care provider." The FTC clarified that it considers the developer of a health app or connected device as a healthcare provider because it "furnishes healthcare services or supplies."

Another significant point the FTC clarified is that vendors of personal health records (PHRs) and PHR-related entities must follow the breach notification procedures outlined in the rule, which include notification of consumers, the FTC, and even the media in some cases. These are not

HIPAA Covered Entities. The updated rule expands the use of electronic notices to consumers, including email notifications in conjunction with other forms of electronic notice, such as text messaging. The notice includes a requirement that any third parties acquiring the information are identified, as are details about the specific data elements included in the breach.

According to the statement, and the definition of a PHR itself, the rule applies to any app that has the technical capacity to draw information from multiple sources, such as from a consumer and an application programming interface (API). What are some examples? The FTC cites a blood sugar monitoring app that receives information entered by the consumer but that also accesses data from the phone, such as the calendar. This means that all those apps that were previously considered exempt, such as fitness trackers, now need to take note.

The second critical aspect of the policy statement pertains to what constitutes a breach. Although most people consider a breach to be an intrusion, ransomware, or an attack by a hacker, the FTC takes a broader view. It has clarified that a breach includes unauthorized access to data, *including sharing of information without an individual's authorization.* This is potentially a very big deal for all those apps that previously fell outside of HIPAA and did not hesitate to share consumer data with advertisers, investor companies, or Big Tech, which often uses such data to build user profiles for activities such as targeted advertising. Those activities using individuals' data, if not authorized by the consumer, are considered a breach, and the FTC has put everyone on notice that more active enforcement of this rule can be expected. The updated rule clarifies that a breach includes both data security breaches as well as unauthorized disclosures. Civil penalties can be up to $43,792 in fines per violation, and violations are handled as a violation of the FTCA as an unfair or deceptive trade practice.

If you are an app developer or own a company involved in developing healthcare apps, you must review the policies, consumer consent and authorizations, and technical controls in place. Evaluate where and how you share consumer data. Look at any data-sharing agreements and contracts where sharing data might be part of the deal. The bottom line is that you need user authorization to share that data. Make sure your team understands the basic requirements as well. One team member who doesn't know their legal duties can create a much larger problem for everyone.

Case in Point: GoodRx

The FTC is demonstrating that it means business. In its first enforcement action taken under the Health Breach Notification Rule, the FTC went after GoodRx for failing to notify consumers of how it was disclosing consumers' personal health information to entities such as Google and Facebook.

GoodRx is a telehealth and prescription discount provider that provided a convenient app for consumers to use. It collects personal health information from users, including information users enter and information gleaned from pharmacy benefit managers when a consumer redeems a GoodRx coupon.

More than 55 million consumers have used the GoodRx app since 2017. The FTC proposed order, filed by the Department of Justice on behalf of the FTC, prohibits GoodRx from sharing user health information with third parties for advertising purposes and has assessed a fine of $1.5 million.[44]

Make sure you review the various rules and regulations that apply to you as well as the guidance put out by the FTC. You can find FTC guidance, enforcement activities, and press releases on the website: ftc.gov. If you're not sure, get help in figuring out which laws and regulations apply to your organization.

It's also important to note that an organization can potentially fall under both HIPAA and this FTC rule. In that case, the FTC is recommending that coordination occur and preferably that the consumer receive the notice from the entity it is familiar with. For instance, if a vendor of an insurance company (therefore, a Business Associate) has a breach, it may be most logical for the insurance company to send out the notice rather than the vendor. Note that the determination of who will notify should be made when any Business Associate Agreements are entered into. The issue of how breaches are managed, including notification, is an important element to include in those agreements.

The Federal Trade Commission Act

The FTC has also used the Federal Trade Commission Act (FTCA) to pursue organizations that fail to secure consumers' sensitive information or that use unfair or deceptive trade practices.

The Federal Trade Commission Act is the primary statute of the commission.[45] Under this act, as amended, the commission is empowered, among other things, to (1) prevent unfair methods of competition and unfair or deceptive acts or practices in or affecting commerce; (2) seek monetary redress and other relief for conduct injurious to consumers; (3) prescribe rules defining with specificity acts or practices that are unfair or deceptive and establishing requirements designed to prevent such acts or practices; (4) gather and compile information and conduct investigations relating to the organization, business, practices, and management of entities engaged in commerce; and (5) make reports and legislative recommendations to Congress and the public.

Case in Point: SkyMed

The FTC found violations of the Federal Trade Commission Act at SkyMed International, when the emergency travel and medical evaluation services company used deceptive practices and failed to secure consumers' private health information.

SkyMed collected consumer information via an online application in order to enroll consumers in a service to provide emergency medical transportation while traveling. Consumers entered their personal health information as part of the application process. On each page of the SkyMed website was a HIPAA logo, which suggested that the company's processes had been reviewed and approved by a government agency, which they had not.

In addition, a researcher discovered the consumer data in an unsecured cloud database. On March 27, 2019, the researcher notified SkyMed that 130,000 member records were able to be accessed. SkyMed did not remedy the problem for over five months, and then it deleted the database without verifying the specific data elements, the identity of exposed consumers, or whether the data had been inappropriately accessed.

The company sent a notice to its plan holders on May 2, 2019, and the notice represented that no sensitive data elements (medical or payment data) were included and that no misuse had been identified.

The FTC cited SkyMed on several issues. First, misrepresentation with respect to the misleading HIPAA logo that suggested government standards/review, which had not actually occurred. Second, deception with respect to the notice. The notice specifically misstated information about the actual data involved and the potential exposure/evaluation done by the company. Last, unfairness to consumers in that the company did not take reasonable measures to protect the security of the information. There was no risk assessment to periodically evaluate the security of the information. There were no security-related policies, procedures, or training for employees in place. There was no process to ensure that old data was deleted when no longer needed. And there was no authentication or other security measures in place.

Note that SkyMed technically met the breach notification requirements (except that it wasn't honest or accurate, but the notice was timely). The egregious nature of the data security practices was, however, found to constitute a violation of the Federal Trade Commission Act. This case serves as a warning of how the FTC can pursue data security lapses as an unfair or deceptive trade practice, and it has been increasingly doing so.

The outcome for SkyMed was an order to perform a number of steps to remediate the matter. SkyMed had to provide consumers with a notice of the action by the FTC and had to implement a very detailed security program. In addition, SkyMed was required to hire external monitors to periodically evaluate its security program and provide reports to the FTC on any incidents as well as attestations of compliance. The actions here are similar to those take by the Office of Inspector General for healthcare providers who run afoul of compliance standards and are put under a Corporate Integrity Agreement. The requirements are typically extensive and result in significant expenditure of time and expense for the company.[46]

In the SkyMed case, the violation was related to data security but also implied misrepresentation due to the use of the HIPAA logo. Note, however, that the FTC is still looking at deceptive trade practices more broadly and will go after marketing and advertising that it believes are misleading.

No matter what products or services your company provides, the following case is an important reminder.

Case in Point: TurboTax

Turbo Tax is obviously not a healthcare company, but this violation is one that could happen to anyone that offers free services that aren't necessarily free or even available to most people.

From the FTC, January 22, 2024:

The Federal Trade Commission has issued an Opinion and Final Order that Intuit Inc., the maker of the popular TurboTax tax filing software, engaged in deceptive advertising in violation of the FTC Act and deceived consumers when it ran ads for "free" tax products and services for which many consumers were ineligible. . . .

The Commission's Final Order prohibits Intuit from advertising or marketing that any good or service is free unless it is free for all consumers or it discloses clearly and conspicuously and in close proximity to the "free" claim the percentage of taxpayers or consumers that qualify for the free product or service. Alternatively, if the good or service is not free for a majority of consumers, it could disclose that a majority of consumers do not qualify.

The order also requires that Intuit disclose clearly and conspicuously all the terms, conditions, and obligations that are required in order to obtain the "free" good or service. If the advertisement is space constrained and not displayed on any TurboTax website, app, email or other company owned or controlled platform, Intuit is not required to include all the terms and conditions in the advertisement itself but must disclose either that a majority of consumers do not qualify for free (if true) or the percentage that do as well as provide a link in such space-constrained online ads that details all the terms and conditions, according to the Commission order.

The order also prohibits Intuit from misrepresenting any material facts about its products or services such as the price, refund policies or consumers' ability to claim a tax credit or deduction or to file their taxes online accurately without using TurboTax's paid service.[47]

90

If you are in the healthcare space, even if you are more on the tech side rather than a provider, you need to be especially careful of the "free" trap. In healthcare, *free* is a red flag for a violation of the Anti-Kickback Statute as well as what we see here flagged by the FTC.

I strongly advise anyone doing marketing for any type of healthcare product or service to review both these FTC cases and to become familiar with the various Anti-Kickback and fraud and abuse healthcare cases, which often come with severe penalties. Review Chapter 6 on fraud and abuse to get more information on the cases and how they might apply to your business.

The Children's Online Privacy Protection Act of 1998

The Children's Online Privacy Protection Act of 1998 (COPPA) might seem less relevant and might not be as frequently at issue as the other laws and regulations discussed here, but it's noteworthy because it addresses operators of websites and online services directed at children younger than 13 years that collect personal information without parental consent. This law, in effect on April 21, 2000, pertains to apps and Internet of Things (IoT) devices, as well, and not only those aimed exclusively at children.

In 2012, the FTC conducted a survey that found many apps included interactive features or shared children's information with third parties without disclosing this to parents.[48] The civil penalties for violations are up to $46,517 per violation. Because this law does not require the apps or sites be solely directed at children, it's one more law to keep in mind that might be applicable to your health app.

Case in Point: Fortnite (Epic Games)

In a recent and record-setting case, Fortnite, created by the video game maker Epic Games, will be paying a $275 million penalty for violating COPPA and an additional $245 million in refunds for tricking users into creating unwanted charges. In addition to financial penalties, Epic is now prohibited from enabling voice and text communications for children and teens without affirmative parental consent.

Although this is a video game and not directly related to health technology, the violations cited by the FTC could happen with apps or websites that collect children's data without parental consent. In the Fortnite case, the default settings that allowed children to text and voice communicate were found to violate the FTCA's prohibition against unfair practices. This case provides a dramatic example of how faulty design (whether by accident or intent) can have drastic consequences.

On top of the privacy concerns, Epic used "dark patterns" to trick players into making unwanted purchases through the use of confusing button configurations, which reportedly led to hundreds of millions of dollars in unauthorized charges.

This case highlights the magnitude of penalties and the types of activities and settings that can give rise to an FTC case.

Conclusion

The FTC has been very active in applying existing laws in new ways and is actively interested in health tech developments. The commission has been aggressively pursuing the various "bad actors" using all the tools in its arsenal.

If you are an app developer or own a company involved in developing healthcare apps, you need to review the policies, consumer consent and authorizations, and technical controls in place at your organization. Evaluate where you share consumer data. Look at any data-sharing agreements and contracts where sharing data might be part of the deal. And review all Business Associate Agreements you have with Covered Entities such as healthcare providers and insurance companies to verify which notifications you've agreed to. If those provisions don't make sense in light of this new guidance, discuss it with the other party and consider updating the BAA.

Make sure you review the various rules and regulations that apply to your organization as well as the various guidance put out by the FTC. You can find guidance, enforcement activities, and press releases on the FTC website.

If you're not sure, get help figuring out which laws and regulations apply to your organization. Similar to other government agencies, the FTC sends out email updates that include key developments, cases, and events. Although nobody likes an overflowing email inbox, I recommend subscribing to the FTC email updates if the commission's laws or enforcement activities seem relevant to your business.

CHAPTER 6
Fraud and Abuse

Who Needs to Read This: All healthcare providers, vendors, and anyone providing services, supplies, or referrals to healthcare organizations; investors in healthcare organizations and start-ups.

In this chapter, I don't focus on only one agency because the fraud and abuse laws are enforced by multiple agencies, although HHS (the Office of the Inspector General [OIG], specifically) is the "front line." In addition, the Department of Justice (DOJ) is often involved, as may be an Assistant US Attorney (AUSA), and there are also fraud and abuse laws at the state level. The government's enforcement is most often aimed at protecting governments healthcare programs, such as Medicare and Medicaid, but there are exceptions, and state laws can be broader.

It's important to understand that you don't have to be intentionally trying to commit a healthcare-related crime to find yourself subject to scrutiny. The False Claims Act has a whistleblower (qui tam) provision that provides a share of the proceeds if an individual reports fraud and abuse and the government decides to intervene in the case. Whistleblowers can be employees, board members, competitors, business partners—anyone who believes that the organization is violating the law. A whistleblower's allegation may not always be correct; but their reports to the government can bring an unwelcome level of scrutiny of the organization. I talk more about whistleblowers in the to-do section at the end of this chapter. Also, intent is not always a requirement to violate a fraud and abuse law-see the Stark section for a strict liability statute.

The terms *fraud, waste,* and *abuse* refer to different types of activities, and I'll start with some clarification:

Fraud is defined as knowingly and willfully executing, or attempting to execute, a scheme or artifice to defraud any healthcare benefit program or to obtain (by means of false or fraudulent pretenses, representations, or promises) any of the money or property owned by, or under the custody or control of, any healthcare benefit program (18 U.S.C. § 1347).

Waste is overutilization of services or other practices that, directly or indirectly, result in unnecessary costs to the healthcare system, including the Medicare and Medicaid programs. Waste is not generally considered to be caused by criminally negligent actions, but by the misuse of resources.

Abuse includes any action or actions that may, directly or indirectly, result in one or more of the following:

- Unnecessary costs to the healthcare system, including the Medicare and Medicaid programs
- Improper payment for services
- Payment for services that fail to meet professionally recognized standards of care
- Services that are medically unnecessary

Abuse involves payment for items or services when there is no legal entitlement to that payment and the healthcare provider or supplier has not knowingly or intentionally misrepresented facts to obtain payment. Identifying abuse isn't always as straightforward as distinguishing fraud, and it requires a review of the facts and circumstances, including the intent of the parties.

Back when compliance programs were initially being established in healthcare, the majority of compliance issues revolved around coding and billing issues. This is clear both in the OIG's *Compliance Program for Individual and Small Group Physician Practices* and in the perspectives of those who were developing programs in those early days. The elements, such as education and training, or conducting internal monitoring, all focused on coding and billing.

The False Claims Act

The False Claims Act (FCA), which was (and still is) the tool most frequently used by the government to pursue healthcare "improprieties," dates all the way back to the days of President Lincoln and was intended to address issues of war profiteering. The FCA has been amended several times, including in 1986, when President Reagan amended the FCA to include greater penalties and to reinstate the qui tam provision that provides rewards for whistleblowers. Penalties now include treble damages, which can result in those massive settlements and fines you see in the news headlines.

In a nutshell the False Claims Act (found at 31 U.S.C. §§ 3729–3733) imposes liability for any person who knowingly submits a false claim to the government or causes another to submit a false claim to the government or knowingly makes a false record or statement to get a false claim paid by the government. Section 3729(a)(1)(G), known as the *reverse false claims section*, provides liability where one acts improperly, not to get money from the government, but to avoid having to pay money to the government. The Department of Justice puts out a good primer on the FCA.[49]

We know that claims that deliberately misstate services or supplies provided are fraudulent and violate the federal False Claims Act. The classic scenarios involve issues such as *upcoding*, where a provider bills for a higher level of services than was provided, or *duplicate billing*, where multiple bills are submitted to secure extra reimbursement for the same service.

The FCA and fraud and abuse laws may not seem relevant to a company that isn't directly billing for healthcare services. This topic is, however, pertinent when it comes to financial relationships and, more recently, cybersecurity and even patient privacy violations by a website developer! Wait, what? See the following Case in Point.

Case in Point: Jelly Bean

This, in March 2023 from the Department of Justice: Jelly Bean Communications Design LLC (Jelly Bean) and Jeremy Spinks have agreed to pay $293,771 to resolve False Claims Act allegations that they failed to secure personal information on a federally funded Florida children's health insurance website, which Jelly Bean created, hosted, and maintained.

"Government contractors responsible for handling personal information must ensure that such information is appropriately protected," said Principal Deputy Assistant Attorney General Brian M. Boynton, head of the Justice Department's Civil Division. "We will use the False Claims Act to hold accountable companies and their management when they knowingly fail to comply with their cybersecurity obligations and put sensitive information at risk."[50]

This is a new use for the False Claims Act, using it both for HIPAA and data privacy violations and for pursuing a case against a website developer who isn't billing the government for healthcare services in the usual sense. This case hasn't gotten much publicity, but in my mind it's a loud warning on expanding the use of the False Claims Act. At this point, you can see that every agency is getting onboard with pursuing privacy and security violation cases, and health tech is right in their cross-hairs.

You should also know that, although I don't have a Case in Point for it yet, cases have been winding their way through the justice system in which violations of the FDA standards have been linked to False Claims Act liability, with the premise being that faulty design or production of devices could, in fact, represent a legitimate FCA claim, where the government was "induced" to authorize a particular product. Check out this document to read the government's view on this issue: *United States' Statement of Interest as to Defendant's Motion to Dismiss* in regard to *United States of America, ex rel. Patricia Crocano, v. Trividia Health Inc.*[51] The Department of Justice asserts that fraud on a federal agency can rise to the level of an FCA violation. From what I've found, the "fraud on the FDA" theory hasn't borne fruit yet but has been debated in the courts and shows how the DOJ views some of these cases.

The False Claims Act is definitely the workhorse law for pursuing a wide range of "bad conduct" in the healthcare space. The cases included in this book, and so many more that you can easily find online, demonstrate the variety of theories and scenarios that can result in FCA liability. And, remember, False Claims Act liability can mean treble damages, which add up very quickly, depending on the facts and what the actual false claims were, and whistleblowers can receive a percentage of any settlement (between 15 percent and 30 percent). Considering that some cases can settle for many millions of dollars, this is a powerful incentive. It's important to understand, too, that these cases can take many years to wind through the judicial system, and a whistleblower can suffer severe professional consequences before ever seeing a payout. Whistleblowing isn't a quick and easy road to travel.

The Anti-Kickback Statute

The Anti-Kickback Statute (AKS) is a criminal statute that basically makes it illegal to pay or receive remuneration for referrals.[52] This may sound straightforward on its face, but sometimes the analysis is complex, particularly when it involves evaluating safe harbors. In addition to potential criminal penalties, civil monetary penalties and exclusion from government healthcare programs are possible.

Specifically, the AKS prohibits a person from knowingly or willfully soliciting, receiving, offering, or paying for any remuneration in return for, or to induce, (1) the referral of patients to receive any items or service for which payment is made under a federal healthcare program, and (2) the purchasing, leasing, ordering, arranging for, or recommending of any such good, facility, item, or service. For the AKS to apply, it is only necessary for "one purpose" of the arrangement to be for wrongfully inducing referrals of government-funded healthcare business. Violations may result in criminal, civil, and administrative penalties (such as exclusion from participating in government healthcare programs).

The term *remuneration*, likewise, is broad and basically includes anything of value.

It's important to have a general understanding of the AKS if you are either a provider (including telehealth) or are providing services or products to providers. For instance, if you are providing medical devices to a provider who participates in federal healthcare programs, be aware that discounts, rebates, or other incentives can be considered a kickback if the item is reimbursed by a government healthcare program. And keep in mind how that item might be reimbursed—is there any way to conceive that the government is paying? It doesn't have to be through direct billing; it can be through cost reports or incentive payments and the like. Any arrangement that involves money and government healthcare programs may be sufficient to be considered reimbursement. This is how the analysis can get complicated.

If you are building a value-based care program, a new telehealth network, or an app to coordinate care, in addition to the "traditional" healthcare arrangements, you need to learn about the AKS, as well as the Stark Law, and be on the lookout for potential problem areas so you can get legal advice. These laws are complex, and this chapter is only a high-level overview that covers the most relevant provisions relating to healthcare technology.

Safe Harbors

A number of safe harbors under the AKS can serve to protect organizations if arrangements are structured to align with a safe harbor. Although, historically, safe harbors were designed for provider arrangements, health tech companies may now find a way to structure arrangements in a safe harbor, and new safe harbors do contemplate the value of digital healthcare technology.

There are many safe harbors; I include here summaries of the ones most likely to be relevant. As always, please consult with an experienced attorney if you are entering into arrangements that could trigger the Anti-Kickback Statute. It's not always straightforward, and it's better to be on the safe side, especially with the enforcement activity ramping up in sometimes unpredictable ways. The following are very brief summaries of the most relevant safe harbors, just to give you a starting point. Also, keep in mind that these safe harbors are changed, or new ones added, from time to time, so stay on top of those updates.

Safe Harbors for the Anti-Kickback Statute

- **Equipment rental.**
- **Personal services and management contracts and outcomes-based payment arrangements.** This commonly used safe harbor requires compensation be set in advance, not based on value or volume of referrals, and memorialized in an agreement no less than one year in duration, among other requirements.

- **Discounts.** Discounts and rebates involve a number of detailed standards to meet safe harbor requirements. Be very careful to ensure compliance when considering a "great deal." This is one of the more complicated safe harbors, in my opinion, and one that is often missed. This one is important if you are considering a deal or want to incentivize buyers of your product or service.
- **Health centers.** This safe harbor exempts the transfer of any goods, items, services, donations or loans (whether the donation or loan is in cash or in-kind), or combination thereof from an individual or entity to a health center as long as the nine standards are met.
- **Electronic prescribing items and services.** Hardware, software, or information technology and training services necessary and used solely to receive and transmit electronic prescription information, if all of the conditions are met, would not be considered remuneration.
- **Electronic health records items and services.** *Remuneration* does not include nonmonetary remuneration (consisting of items and services in the form of software or information technology and training services, including cybersecurity software and services) necessary and used predominantly to create, maintain, transmit, receive, or protect electronic health records if all of the applicable conditions are met.
- **Care coordination arrangements to improve quality, health outcomes, and efficiency.** This safe harbor applies to participants in value-based enterprises (VBEs), which can include providers of digital health tools and services.
- **Arrangements for patient engagement and support to improve quality, health outcomes, and efficiency.** This safe harbor refers to patient engagement tools or support furnished by a value-based enterprise (VBE) participant for eligible patients. Note that providers of digital health technology may be part of a VBE and should do additional research to better understand how they can take advantage

99

of this safe harbor as well as the care coordination safe harbor above. HHS defines *digital health technology* as "hardware, software, or services that electronically capture, transmit, aggregate, or analyze data and that are used for the purpose of coordinating and managing care."

- **Cybersecurity technology and related services.** Nonmonetary remuneration consisting of cybersecurity technology and services used predominantly to implement, maintain, or reestablish effective cybersecurity.

This is a very abbreviated list of safe harbors because my intent is to provide a high-level overview to get you started in evaluating potential arrangements. No matter what deal you are contemplating, however, certain truths apply:

- Arrangements should always be signed and in writing for best protection.
- Reimbursement must not be based on volume or value of referrals.
- The agreement needs to specify the compensation, or payments, set in advance.
- The arrangement must be commercially reasonable, that is, it makes business sense regardless of payments.
- The compensation must be Fair Market Value. You should have a policy and procedure related to Fair Market Value that shows how you make that determination.

My view is that if you are contemplating entering an arrangement for products or services, get bids or offers from several potential business partners and have a process for objectively selecting from among them. You don't want the OIG to think that you chose your significant other's sister-in-law's cybersecurity company for any reason other than pure merit. Even if you don't think the Anti-Kickback Statute would apply, it's a good idea to get guidance because both referrals and remuneration can be less than obvious to many people, given past cases and interpretation by the government and the courts.

One of the primary areas where enormous cases relating to the Anti-Kickback Statute have been settled is pharmaceuticals. These cases are so many variations on a theme: Basically, they involve pharmaceutical companies paying physicians or healthcare providers to use or promote their products. In addition to the kickback issue, many of the pharma companies get in trouble for off-label marketing, which occurs when a drug is not approved for a specific use by the Food and Drug Administration (FDA), but the drug company promotes it for that use anyway. In many cases, the pharmaceutical companies have paid physicians to promote their medications for off-label use, thus resulting in a kickback case and an off-label marketing case.

It's important to note that medical device companies have also been liable for similar issues, so the pharma cases are important to understand even if you're on the device side, *keeping in mind that healthcare technology and software can also be considered devices.* That means these cases can have broader applicability than you might initially think.

These cases have settled in amounts of hundreds of millions of dollars and have sparked a whole new area of focus for not only government investigations but also compliance program activities.

If you're on the provider side of healthcare, you need to monitor relationships with pharmaceutical and medical suppliers, as well as various tech vendors and developers, as part of your compliance responsibilities. Any situation in which someone—whether a pharmaceutical or device manufacturer, a clinical laboratory, or some other individual who may make or receive referrals—is giving or receiving something of value, it needs to fit within a specific safe harbor. A kickback can come in many forms: tickets to a sporting event, a trip to a conference or other industry event, a lease for which the rate is not based on Fair Market Value, or the exchange of discounts/free items or services between the parties to an arrangement, among others.

When the huge pharmaceutical cases emerged and the industry responded, many healthcare providers and other organizations tightened their policies. Some took a very conservative approach and banned gifts and meals altogether. Others, however, have deeply ingrained practices and cultures, and you will face challenges in getting practitioners to say goodbye to their free tickets to sporting events and other goodies.

One key message to convey when you are talking to physicians, leaders, and employees about kickback risks is to explain that under the law both the party that gives and the party that receives may be found liable. Yes, the drug and device companies have taken a huge hit. But physicians have been prosecuted too, as have CEOs and board members. The government has made it quite clear that it is looking for individual culpability when an organization gets in trouble, so people need to understand their risk if they engage in these behaviors.

The other issue that I think is very important for tech companies and providers to understand is discounts. I know that nobody wants to pay more than they have to, or incur legal fees, but discounts (and free goods or services, of course) can be construed as kickbacks, and you want to evaluate any proposed arrangement carefully.

Consider a device company that offers free iPads to all providers when their organization buys the company's health tech service or product. The iPads can be used to access electronic medical records (EMRs), which is a benefit to the practice, but the devices clearly confer many other benefits on the users. (Note: Free items that can *only* be used with the purchased product are usually viewed as acceptable.) The OIG would likely consider this to be a kickback situation because iPads are not items that can be used only with the purchased product but also provide personal benefits. The physicians, however, can make a very heartfelt appeal about the many benefits to patients and time-saving features. Despite a convincing explanation, the OIG likely would not see this as an appropriate "freebie."

Such offers can be tempting to an organization, and that's the whole point, right? The cost of a tablet, for instance, in a small practice is obviously a larger percentage of the budget than it is for a large hospital. The same argument applies when a vendor offers to pay for trips to conferences where physicians can earn their continuing medical education credits. An out-of-town conference can easily cost $3,000 to $5,000 or more per person. It's not at all difficult to understand a physician's desire to attend. It isn't that the physician is looking for a free trip (they may or may not be) but that the expense won't accrue to the practice or be a personal cost to the physician. Many pharmaceutical and device companies have quit offering these goodies, however, after all the expensive settlements and the advent of industry guidance by pharma, AdvaMed, and others, as outlined in Chapter 7 on industry guidance.

With the rapid increase in healthcare technology and a lack of applicable laws, you will see that the old standby False Claims Act is being used creatively against health tech companies. The FCA has often been bootstrapped to the Stark and Anti-Kickback laws, but recently it was used for HIPAA violations by a website developer, as described in the Jelly Bean Case in Point earlier. So beware, as laws and regulations work to catch up, there may be some inventive applications of the existing laws to curb behavior the government deems unlawful or harmful.

Case in Point: Modernizing Medicine

In November 2022, Modernizing Medicine agreed to pay $45 million to resolve allegations of accepting and paying illegal kickbacks and causing false claims.

Modernizing Medicine Inc. (ModMed), an electronic health record (EHR) technology vendor located in Boca Raton, Florida, has agreed to pay $45 million to resolve allegations that it violated the False Claims Act (FCA) by accepting and providing unlawful remuneration in exchange for referrals and by causing its users to report inaccurate information in connection with claims for federal incentive payments.

The Anti-Kickback Statute prohibits anyone from offering or paying, directly or indirectly, any remuneration—which includes money or any other thing of value—to induce referrals of items or services covered by Medicare, Medicaid and other federally funded programs. In a complaint filed in conjunction with today's settlement, the United States alleged that ModMed violated the FCA and the Anti-Kickback Statute through three marketing programs: First, ModMed solicited and received kickbacks from Miraca Life Sciences Inc. (Miraca) in exchange for recommending and arranging for ModMed's users to utilize Miraca's pathology lab services. Second, ModMed conspired with Miraca to improperly donate ModMed's EHR to health care providers in an effort to increase lab

---

orders to Miraca and simultaneously add customers to ModMed's user base. Third, ModMed paid kickbacks to its current health care provider customers and to other influential sources in the health-care industry to recommend ModMed's EHR and refer potential customers to ModMed.

"Electronic health records serve a critical role in informing physician decision making, and it is therefore essential that health care providers select such technology free from the influence of improper financial inducements," said Principal Deputy Assistant Attorney General Brian M. Boynton, head of the Department of Justice's Civil Division. **"Vendors of electronic health records will be held to the same standards of compliance that we expect of everyone who provides health care services"** [emphasis mine].

"Today's settlement marks the fourth resolution that our office has achieved as we seek to root out fraud in the electronic health record technology field," said U.S. Attorney Nikolas P. Kerest for the District of Vermont. "It is imperative that medical providers be able to trust the health record systems with which they document important and sensitive patient information, and for too long electronic health record vendors have prioritized only sales. The government alleges that for years, ModMed, through a variety of schemes, engaged in illegal kickbacks that distorted both the EMR and pathology lab markets, in addition to providing its users with a deficient product. This resolution reflects the seriousness of the government's allegations and the determination of the Department of Justice to restore integrity to the electronic health record field."

As a result of this conduct, the government alleges that ModMed improperly generated sales for itself and for Miraca, while causing health care providers to submit false claims for reimbursement to the federal government for pathology services, and for incentive payments from the Department of Health and Human Services (HHS) for the adoption and "meaningful use" of ModMed's EHR technology.

In January 2019, Miraca (now known as Inform Diagnostics) agreed to pay $63.5 million to resolve allegations that it violated the Anti-Kickback Statute and the Stark Law by providing to referring physicians subsidies for EHR systems and free or discounted technology consulting services.

Additionally, under HHS' EHR Incentive Programs, HHS offered incentive payments to health care providers that adopted certified EHR technology and met certain requirements relating to their "meaningful use" of that technology. Eligibility for incentive payments required health care providers to use certified EHR technology that, among other things, utilized certain standard vocabularies for drugs (RxNorm) and clinical terminology (SNOMED CT) in order to conduct certain transactions. The government's complaint in intervention alleges that ModMed knew that its EHR did not always allow physician users to electronically record medical records using the required standard vocabularies, thereby causing certain of its users to submit false claims for incentive payments under that program.[53]

A few key points to note regarding the Modernizing Medicine case: First, consistent with recent guidance by the government, the Department of Justice joined the case against the two founders and executives of the company. This is significant because the government has stated repeatedly that it will pursue cases against executives, founders, and board members in fraud and abuse and other cases.

In addition, one of the reasons this case was considered under the FCA was that the EHR usage was tied to Meaningful Use incentive payments. Remember when I said that you had to look beyond direct billing for healthcare technology services or supplies? Improper referrals to use the system (including cash and gift card payments) were made, and the EHR system was also set up to funnel diagnostic laboratory testing to Miraca. Payments made by government healthcare programs were therefor implicated.

The biggest takeaway for me is the statement I emphasized within the Department of Justice announcement: "Vendors of electronic health records will be held to the same standards of compliance that we expect of everyone who provides health care services." Gone are the days when vendors engaged in various marketing schemes unnoticed. The bigger question now is which of the alphabet-soup agencies will go after them?

The Stark Law

The Stark Law is also known as the *physician self-referral statute*, which gives you an idea of what it is about. *Physician self-referral* is when a physician refers a patient to medical services in which the physician has a financial interest, which could be ownership, investment, or a structured compensation arrangement. Although Stark began as a self-referral prohibition for clinical laboratory services for Medicare beneficiaries, it ultimately expanded to include a broad range of health services (designated health services, or DHS).

The Stark Law is narrower than the Anti-Kickback Statute to the extent that it applies only to physicians. There are a number of exceptions for different types of physician arrangements, but to get protection under an exception, the arrangement does need to be structured in accordance with the exception requirements. Close doesn't cut it.

Some of the more common exceptions to Stark include arrangements such as personal services, employment, and leases. Exception requirements under Stark are similar to those of the Anti-Kickback Statute: The arrangement must be set out in writing, and the terms need to be for Fair Market Value, without respect to volume or value of referrals, and commercially reasonable. In other words, the arrangement should make sense even if there are no referrals flowing, which may seem counterintuitive—if there is no benefit, why would you enter into the arrangement? That's why it's important to meet the criteria, including demonstrating the need for that service or arrangement to address patient care needs.

Stark is very complex, and it is necessary to have a good Stark attorney as a resource. Physician arrangements need to be reviewed by counsel. If your practice uses a standard agreement, whether for physician employment or for independent contractors, counsel should review and approve the template.

In the past, organizations self-disclosed identified "technical" Stark violations. These violations included arrangements such as expired contracts or contracts that neither party had actually signed. Sometimes self-audits revealed that small payments were made to physicians with no contract whatsoever in place. These types of violations usually resulted from sloppiness or lack of understanding rather than any intent to "self-refer." The problem, however, is that Stark is a strict liability statute. A strict liability statute is one in which intent doesn't matter. That is why the organizations that discovered these seemingly minor issues had to disclose to the government.

These types of arrangements and cases are important to be aware of if you are an actual healthcare service provider. But what if you are a technology company? We saw earlier that the DOJ pursued a case against a web developer for privacy violations under the False Claims Act. Yes, that's data privacy again, not "actual" fraud and abuse. Although there are many examples of creative applications of the False Claims Act and the FTCA, Stark is geared toward a more specific issue: physician self-referrals. If you don't have a physician in your organization, this is one law you have less need to worry about.

About Those Whistleblowers

We hear now and then about huge "windfall" whistleblower cases, cases like Enron's or some of the pharmaceutical companies', where the settlements were massive for cases brought by a qui tam relator or whistleblower. It's an organization's worst nightmare: one of their employees or business partners reporting them to the government and triggering an investigation.

A whistleblower first has to get an attorney with expertise in these cases. This helps preserve confidentiality and ensures the case is appropriate, with necessary documentation to submit to the government. The government will decide whether or not to intervene. Only about 25 percent of qui tam cases are accepted, although the relator can still proceed with the case. The case is sealed until the government decides to intervene, at which point the allegations and relator become public information.

Most whistleblowers tried reporting their concerns internally before going to the government. This is crucial to know because it's a key to reducing organizational risk. Despite the potential for massive payouts, in reality such cases are rare and the impact on the relator's life can be extremely disruptive and even traumatic as the case drags on and the relator is subject to a range of professional consequences. It isn't an easy choice to make to be a whistleblower, is my point.

Given all that, what can an organization do to protect itself? First, of course, become familiar with the fraud and abuse laws, industry guidance, and the basic compliance program requirements that provide a framework for training and education, monitoring risk areas, and reporting concerns. If an organization is doing everything "right," the risk of a relator is quite small. There are, however, people who will truly believe you are doing something wrong and can't be dissuaded. Your compliance program will serve you well in that situation, because you will have processes set up requiring employees to report concerns and a corresponding procedure for the investigation of such concerns.

Whistleblowers are generally made, not born. In addition to the compliance program, there is the human component to all this. You might have an employee who constantly believes things are being done incorrectly. They see fraud everywhere they look and don't hesitate to send emails around using that particular "F word." It is easy to become aggravated and seek to ignore the noise from this person. That's the type of mistake that creates relators, and that annoying person may be right some of the time, or even just once. Once is enough.

Make sure you have a true open-door policy and that it is extended to those challenging employees. Document the person's concerns and look into them. Once you've done that, be sure to respond to the employee and let them know what you can about your review (keeping in mind confidentiality of other employees who may have been disciplined). If he or she believes you've listened to the concern and taken appropriate action, they are much less likely to take it any further.

One other related issue to be aware of is retaliation. *Retaliation* is any adverse employment-related action taken as a result of an employee reporting a concern or cooperating in an investigation. What that means, in reality, is that you can't start excluding that person from meetings, changing their shift, or doing other things to keep them from further discussing or reporting. Retaliation isn't just firing or disciplinary action. Also, if that person is a member of a protected class, the issue is compounded. Make sure your management team understands this. If organizations did a better job encouraging employees to report, and then following up appropriately, there would be far fewer whistleblowers.

To-Do List

Providers: If you are a provider of healthcare services, whether live or via telehealth, make sure your referral arrangements, physician compensation, and marketing activities don't cross any lines that could be construed as fraud or abuse. Contracts and referral arrangements, in particular, should be reviewed by legal counsel with expertise in this area.

Health tech developers, manufacturers, and vendors: If you are a developer, manufacturer, or vendor of health-related technology, you need to be aware of privacy and security requirements as you develop your product and, of course, any FDA approvals if the device requires it. Aren't we talking about fraud and abuse? Yes, but we've seen the False Claims Act bootstrapped to cybersecurity and other "tech" shortcomings.

Once you've gone through the appropriate steps in developing a secure and approved product, make sure you have the proper notices and consents for data usage, and make sure the patient's or consumer's data is not being transferred to and is not accessible by third-party organizations. Don't enter into any referral arrangements without talking to legal counsel, and have counsel assist you if you are considering any discounts, rebates, or other "deals" with healthcare practices. Last, your marketing has to be honest, including any representations about the security of your systems.

Everyone: Put a compliance program in place to ensure that employees are all trained on fraud and abuse and to create a mechanism for self-auditing. Make sure you have a robust and well-publicized process for employees to report concerns and that you and your team follow up consistently. If you do end up with a problem, you have the ability to correct it yourself rather than after the government gets involved. This also minimizes the risk of a relator.

Conclusion

The healthcare fraud and abuse laws are complex, and the situational facts are key to determining compliance. Although I strongly encourage everyone to have a healthcare fraud and abuse attorney as a resource, I think it's vital to review cases that are relevant to your business or practice and monitor government guidance and updates. Your goal should be to have a basic understanding so that you know when it is necessary to contact legal counsel.

CHAPTER 7
Industry Compliance Guidance

Who Needs to Read This: Developers and manufacturers of medical devices; providers dealing with device, pharmaceutical, or software manufacturers.

I have included this chapter following the fraud and abuse chapter because the industry guidance documents referenced herein provide very specific details for compliance with those laws.

Whether you are developing "regulated" devices or software or are dealing with companies that are, this industry guidance provides a road map to your risk areas and the standards for addressing them. The Medical Device Manufacturers Association of America (MDMA), the Advanced Medical Technology Association (AdvaMed), and the Pharmaceutical Research and Manufacturers of America (PhRMA) have each developed guidance based on enforcement activities taken by the federal government. The Anti-Kickback Statute, Stark laws, and False Claims Act are all tools in the government's arsenal to curtail the previous culture of drug and device companies "wining and dining" physicians and other prescribers.

At first blush, you may think this doesn't pertain to you. Perhaps you are a software developer or setting up a telehealth practice. Although your line of business may not be one of the segments of the industry targeted when these documents were created, don't dismiss them too quickly. As noted elsewhere in this book, the FDA considers a wide range of new technologies as medical devices, for example. If you are setting up a healthcare practice of any type that will interact with suppliers or vendors, these documents are helpful for understanding which offers, deals, and freebies do not run afoul of the applicable fraud and abuse laws.

Just keep in mind that these guidance documents were born out of multimillion-dollar settlements and fines. It is in your best interest to at least glance at the components that could apply to your business and consider sharing the information with anyone on your team who could also be impacted.

Case in Point: Athena

In case you're not yet convinced, read this case from 2021:

A national electronic health records (EHR) technology vendor based in Watertown, Massachusetts, athenahealth Inc. (Athena), has agreed to pay $18.25 million to resolve allegations that it violated the False Claims Act by paying unlawful kickbacks to generate sales of its EHR product, athenaClinicals, the Justice Department announced today.

In a complaint filed in conjunction with today's settlement, the United States alleged that Athena violated the False Claims Act and the Anti-Kickback Statute through three marketing programs. First, Athena invited prospective and existing customers to "Concierge Events," providing free tickets to and amenities at sporting, entertainment, and recreational events, including trips to the Masters Tournament and the Kentucky Derby with complimentary travel and luxury accommodations, meals, and alcohol. Second, Athena paid kickbacks to its existing customers under a "Lead Generation" program designed to identify and refer new prospective clients to Athena. Under this program, Athena paid up to $3,000 to existing customers for each new client that signed up for Athena services, regardless of how much time, if any, the existing customer spent speaking to or meeting with the new client. Finally, Athena entered into deals with competing vendors that were discontinuing their EHR technology offerings to refer their clients to Athena. Under such deals, Athena paid remuneration to the competitor based on the value and volume of practices that were successfully converted into Athena clients.

"This resolution demonstrates the department's continued commitment to hold EHR companies accountable for the payment of unlawful kickbacks in any form," said Acting Assistant Attorney General Brian Boynton for the Department of Justice's Civil Division. "EHR technology plays an important role in the provision of medical care, and it is critical that the selection of an EHR platform be made without the influence of improper financial inducements."

"Across the country, physicians rely on electronic health records software to provide vital patient data. Kickbacks corrupt the market for health care services and risk jeopardizing patient safety," said U.S. Attorney Andrew E. Lelling for the District of Massachusetts. "We will aggressively pursue organizations that fail to play by the rules; EHR companies are no exception."[54]

This is the perfect case to launch into the industry guidance to show how marketing activities and referral arrangements can result in a whole lot of trouble for those who don't follow appropriate business practices. Not only that, but activities that may have been accepted in times past are now taboo, so it really is important to monitor the changes and updates to laws, cases, and industry guidance.

Below I summarize the key provisions of the Medical Device Manufacturers Association's guidance document because MDMA is very involved in the healthcare technology space. The other guidance documents from AdvaMed and PhRMA are similar. It would be useful for you to review any of the three, along with the fraud and abuse laws, as you build your processes and enter into various business relationships.

Appropriate Conduct in Interactions with Healthcare Professionals

The Medical Device Manufacturers Association of America (MDMA) has developed "Code of Conduct on Interactions with Healthcare Providers" that specifically applies to its members (defined as manufacturers of medical devices, diagnostic products, or healthcare information systems who are members of MDMA), but this is also useful guidance whether you fit on

113

the provider side or the manufacturer side of the equation.

The main thrust of these industry documents is to guide marketing and financial arrangements between manufacturers and healthcare providers. There is a solid reason for this emphasis: The government has targeted such financial arrangements, particularly in the pharmaceutical industry, as violations of the Anti-Kickback Statute and False Claims Act.

Although complying with this guidance is purely voluntary, it is a good idea to carefully consider it when developing your own practices. I recommend you pull one of these documents for yourself and use it as a policy development tool. Please note that I have included an abbreviated version of the document here, and it is not a word-for-word reiteration. I've included the sections related to the issues that arise most frequently. If you want a more in-depth and detailed read, reference the online version.

Here are the key topics and the recommended practices. Again, this is my high-level summary. If you are planning any of these activities and think you might run into risky territory, do a close review of the original documents and, if you're still not sure, get help from a legal or compliance professional who works with this subject matter.

I use the word *vendor* here to represent companies on the manufacturing or development side so they get an idea of how to structure relationships with their healthcare clients and customers.

Product Training and Education

One of the big areas of government enforcement has been "boondoggle events," where vendors invite providers to lavish events at exotic locations and call it "education." It is acceptable for vendors to provide education, but it needs to be at a modest location that is conducive to learning. Meals are acceptable, again, if modest.

Supporting Third-Party Educational Conferences

It is generally acceptable to sponsor a healthcare provider attending a bona fide educational or scientific conference as long as it's an accredited continuing education event. If the event is appropriate, the vendor can provide a grant to the conference organizer. The same is true for meals as long as the vendor cannot pick and choose which recipients receive the benefit, that is, it would benefit all attendees. Generally, benefits are not provided for spouses or guests.

Support for healthcare providers in training is also acceptable provided that the grants are to the training institution and the vendor isn't choosing recipients.

Advertisements and Demonstrations

Vendors may purchase advertising, exhibit space, and other promotional arrangements as long as they are commercially reasonable and meet the applicable standards.

Speaker Arrangements

When allowed, vendors may select and send faculty to speak at third-party conferences provided that the arrangement is documented in a consulting agreement (unless the speaker is an employee of the vendor). The speaker must also disclose to attendees that he or she is presenting on behalf of, and paid by, the vendor.

No Direct Sponsorship

Vendors may not contribute directly (whether in cash or in-kind) to the costs of registration, travel, or lodging to send an individual healthcare provider to a third-party conference. The only exceptions are when the situation fits one of the other allowed arrangements, such as a consulting arrangement or a product training.

Business Meetings

Members may conduct sales or other business meetings with healthcare providers, but the setting must be conducive to business and any meals or other expenses must be modest and reasonable.

Consulting Arrangements with Healthcare Providers

There are a variety of legitimate reasons why a manufacturer or developer might bring in a healthcare provider as a consultant. It's important that the arrangement be for a legitimate purpose and that the provider is reimbursed at Fair Market Value. Because these arrangements can be high risk, vendors should adhere to the following guidance, which tracks with requirements of the Anti-Kickback and Stark laws:

- Consulting agreements should be written and should describe all services to be provided.
- There needs to be a legitimate business need for the arrangements.
- The consultant should be selected on the basis of the consultant's relevant qualifications and expertise and not as a reward for past usage or as an unlawful inducement for future purchases. The vendor should have an objective selection process that is documented and followed.
- Compensation paid to a consultant should be consistent with Fair Market Value in an arm's-length transaction for the services provided. Fair Market Value should be based on objective criteria and should not be based on the volume or value of the consultant's past, present, or anticipated business.
- A vendor may pay for documented, reasonable, and actual expenses incurred by a consultant that are necessary to carry out the consulting arrangement, such as costs for travel, meals, and lodging.
- Meetings with consultants should be appropriate to the subject matter of the agreement and should be held in a neutral setting conducive to business, clinical, or educational discussions.
- Vendor-sponsored meals and refreshments provided in conjunction with a consultant meeting should be reasonable in value and should be subordinate in time and focus to the primary purpose of the meeting. Vendors should not provide recreation or entertainment in conjunction with these meetings.
- A vendor's sales personnel may provide input about the qualifications of a proposed consultant, but sales personnel

should not control or unduly influence the decision to engage a particular healthcare provider as a consultant.

Prohibition on Entertainment and Recreation

Health tech companies and manufacturers should only support activities with healthcare providers that are professional in nature and that serve only to enhance patient care. It is not appropriate for vendors to pay for any entertainment or recreational event or activity for any healthcare provider. Such activities include, for example, theater, sporting events, golf, skiing, hunting, sporting equipment, and leisure or vacation trips.

Meals Associated with Healthcare Provider Business Interactions

Modest meals may be provided to healthcare providers in conjunction with business, scientific, or educational events as an occasional business courtesy consistent with the following limitations:

- *Purpose.* The meal should be incidental to the bona fide discussion of scientific, educational, or business information and should be provided in a manner conducive to the discussion of such information. Meals should be subordinate in time and focus to the purpose of the meeting or event. The meal should not be part of an entertainment or recreational event.
- *Setting and Location.* Meals should be in a setting that is conducive to bona fide scientific, educational, or business discussions. Meals may occur at the healthcare provider's place of business or in another location (such as a restaurant or conference room) that is conducive to the discussion.
- *Participants.* Meals may be provided only to healthcare providers who actually attend and have a bona fide purpose for attending the meeting. Meals may not be provided for other office staff, spouses, or guests and may not be provided if the representative is not present (such as a "dine & dash" program).

117

Prohibition on Personal Gifts

A vendor occasionally may provide educational items to healthcare providers that benefit patients or serve a genuine educational function for healthcare providers. Other than medical textbooks and anatomical models, any such item should have a Fair Market Value of less than $100. Prohibited items include items for the recipient's personal or business use and personal gifts such as holiday gifts, wine, or cash.

Research and Educational Grants and Charitable Donations

A vendor may provide research and educational grants and charitable donations to entities or organizations with a genuine scientific, educational, or charitable mission or function as long as they are not being provided as an unlawful inducement. Ensure that objective criteria are in place and that those standards are consistently followed. No grant or donations should ever be made on the basis of the volume or value of purchases or anticipated future purchases. Always keep documentation of both the decision-making process and the distribution.

Research Grants

A vendor may provide research grants to support independent medical research with scientific merit. Such activities should have well-defined objectives and milestones and may not be linked directly or indirectly to the purchase of vendor products or technologies. Grants should be made pursuant to written grant requests from the proposed recipient, including a protocol describing the proposed activity and its objectives, milestones, and timeline; a budget for the research project; and requirements (if any) for third-party authorizations (including institutional or regulatory approvals). Both monetary and in-kind grants should be appropriately documented (for example, by a written agreement between the vendor and the recipient). Recipients of research grants should maintain independent control over the research.

Educational Grants

Educational grants may be provided for legitimate purposes, including, but not limited to, the advancement of medical education or public education. The grantor cannot select or influence the selection of the individual recipient of grant benefits.

Charitable Donations

A vendor may make monetary or product donations for charitable purposes, such as supporting indigent care, patient education, public education, or the sponsorship of events where the proceeds are intended for charitable purposes. Donations should be motivated by bona fide charitable purposes and should be made only to nonprofit organizations with a bona fide charitable or philanthropic purpose. When donating free products, vendors should require the recipient to agree not to charge a third party for the products.

Evaluation and Demonstration Products, Product Consignment

Providing products to healthcare providers at no charge for evaluation or demonstration purposes can benefit patients by improving patient care and safety. Certain products may be provided to healthcare providers at no charge for evaluation and demonstration purposes under certain circumstances. These products may be provided at no charge to allow healthcare providers to assess the appropriate use and functionality of the product and determine whether and when to use, order, purchase, or recommend the product in the future. Vendor products provided for evaluation are typically expected to be used in patient care.

Whenever vendors provide free or loaned products and equipment, they must comply with applicable transparency reporting laws and regulations.

Technical Support in Clinical Setting

Healthcare providers may require or request product support, such as guidance on the technical controls and functionality of a product. Vendor representatives should be present only at the request of and under the supervision of a healthcare provider when providing product support in a clinical setting and should always comply with applicable policies and procedures of the clinical facility, including vendor credentialing requirements, as well as policies and procedures designed to protect patient privacy. Vendor representatives should be transparent that they are acting on behalf of the company in a technical support capacity. Member representatives should not interfere with the clinical decision-making of healthcare providers and should not provide support that eliminates any overhead or other expenses that a healthcare provider would otherwise incur while providing clinical care to patients.

Joint Education and Marketing with Healthcare Providers

Vendors may collaborate with healthcare providers in educational or marketing activities designed to promote both the vendor's products and/or services and the services or facilities of the healthcare provider. Vendors should engage in such activities only when they have a bona fide, legitimate need to engage in the activity for their own educational or marketing purposes, and they should implement controls to help ensure that such arrangements are not made with an intent to provide an improper inducement. These arrangements should include the following requirements:

- The vendor and the healthcare provider should contribute equitably to the conduct and costs of the activity.
- The arrangements should be documented in a written agreement between the vendor and the healthcare provider.
- The program or activity should be balanced and promote both the vendor's medical technologies and the healthcare provider's services and/or facilities.
- The vendor should require participating healthcare providers to comply with applicable company guidelines, including on providing information related to a product's labeling and furnishing appropriate reimbursement and health economics information.

Travel and Lodging Arrangements

Vendors may only arrange or pay for travel or lodging for healthcare providers in a manner that does not constitute an unlawful inducement or create a perception of impropriety. Vendors should adopt policies to ensure the following:

- There must be an objective, legitimate reason for out-of-town travel, such as the need to deliver product-related training and education or the inability to effectively deliver the content through means other than an in-person meeting. Vendors are encouraged to document the legitimate need for travel.

- Travel and lodging arrangements may be provided only as reasonably required in connection with the need for which travel is being arranged and should correspond to the duration for which the individual's attendance is required.

- Vendors may not pay additional travel or lodging costs of a spouse or guest traveling or staying with a healthcare professional.

- Travel and lodging arrangements should be modest and reasonable under the circumstances.

- Vendors should select meeting and lodging locations and venues that are convenient, accessible, and suitable for the business purpose of the meeting. They should not select a meeting or lodging location or venue on the basis of entertainment or recreational value and should not select top-category or luxury hotels or resort facilities unless a reasonable justification supports such venues (in which case vendors are encouraged to document the reason for the venue).

- Vendors should be aware that other laws or regulations may apply to paying for healthcare professionals' travel and lodging, including potentially more restrictive state laws.

AdvaMed, an industry group that represents medical products, technologies, and services manufacturers, created a similar guidance document for its members titled *Code of Ethics on Interactions with Health Care Professionals*.[55]

Free Resource Alert: AdvaMed has a robust (and free) toolkit that includes presentations and training tools that address fraud and abuse risks, international corruption issues, financial recordkeeping controls, and more. The Global Distributor Compliance Toolkit is available through the members-only website but can be accessed without a membership. Go to Advamed.org, and type *Compliance* into the search function. You will find the AdvaMed Code of Ethics, the Global Distributor Compliance Toolkit, and a variety of other valuable resources. I highly recommend checking out this resource for its many good articles and information that relate to healthcare technology.

Conclusion

With the increased merging of technology with more traditional healthcare products and services, it's important to stay abreast of the regulators' and industry's application of previous laws, guidance, and enforcement. In the past, a healthcare software developer would likely never have read the guidance produced by MGMA or AdvaMed, but with so much new technology being classified as regulated medical devices, and with regulators looking for ways to apply the existing laws, the best plan is for developers to be familiar with industry guidance.

The fundamental safeguards and compliance strategies you'll find in the industry documents mentioned here are well worth considering, especially as you monitor enforcement activity and see how the various fraud and abuse laws are being applied in new ways. I recommend reviewing these standards and keeping them in mind as you create policies, procedures, and training for your teams or other associates.

PART III

Compliance

CHAPTER 8

Compliance Programs for Health Tech Companies

Who Needs to Read This: Healthcare organizations and organizations providing services or products to healthcare providers and organizations.

The Health and Human Services Office of the Inspector General (OIG) has identified seven elements of a robust compliance program. As you evaluate your organization's need for a compliance program, it's important you understand which risk exposures the organization faces and how to design the compliance program to cover those areas and what that entails. If your organization develops and provides health technology to providers and health plans, you should be familiar with the current regulatory framework for protecting PHI so that compliance is built in to your products, but your own company's compliance program may be relatively lightweight.

What if your organization is not only providing technology but also has a direct role in patient care? If that is the case, then your compliance responsibilities just grew exponentially. Maybe you are a telehealth provider or are providing mobile lab services or nursing care, and you've developed an app that schedules, tracks, or deploys those services. If that is the case, you need to design a full-scale compliance program, particularly if you are billing any government programs for those services.

Even if you are not billing the government, there are certain things to be mindful of on the front end of your endeavor. At a minimum, you need a solid evaluation of the services you offer, who you contract with, and which aspects of your business present a compliance risk. From there, you can design a compliance program that addresses your risk areas. Also be mindful of the scope of the government's reach—you can find yourself subject to compliance with fraud, abuse, and other laws by virtue of any remuneration you receive from the government (not necessarily direct billing/reimbursement for services or products) or who you contract with. It isn't always as straightforward as you might think (or hope).

The OIG has issued guidance documents for different sectors of healthcare that provide useful road maps for healthcare organizations. But, as I mentioned earlier, the regulatory framework has not caught up with the technology now being developed, so you won't find an OIG compliance guidance document for healthcare technology or telehealth companies and providers.

What you will find are guidance documents pertaining to compliance for home services, small physician practices, and billing companies, among many others. These three forms of guidance can give you good insight into areas of compliance risk and the types of controls expected no matter which health technology services you provide or use.

If you do not provide any patient care and are not billing government healthcare programs, your compliance responsibilities lay primarily in the regulatory areas outlined earlier, that is, HIPAA, the FDA, and the FTC. Although the assertion in the previous sentence may make you think you're off the hook, remember that regulators expect organizations to adhere to laws and regulations in a way that mimics compliance program requirements, including implementing policies and procedures, training, auditing and monitoring, and managing breaches and other incidents. In fact, the HIPAA regulations include all of these elements and many more. When you think about compliance programs, it's best to think of them as a framework for ensuring your organization is covering all the necessary activities for following the applicable laws and regulations. For each of the seven elements of a compliance program, consider the applicable laws and what you need to do in that section.

If you do provide healthcare services, particularly to patients of government healthcare programs (Medicare, Medicaid, SCHIP, Tricare, etc.), then this chapter is pertinent to you. Keep in mind throughout that compliance programs are scalable. The OIG specifically notes this point, and there is no expectation that a very small provider or start-up organization would invest in its compliance program at the same level as a large hospital would. Each requirement of a compliance program can be met without investing an unreasonable amount of time and money. My goal here is to help you identify ways to meet the requirements without a heavy investment of time or capital.

One benefit of having a compliance program is being able to answer insurance companies', investors', and potential clients' inquiries about what you are doing with respect to compliance. If your organization is primarily technology-based and does not provide patient care, you can answer such inquiries by showing that your organization complies with HIPAA, which requires the seven compliance program elements, and other relevant data security laws and industry standards. To the extent other requirements apply, such as FDA approvals, of course you will be expected to show that as well, and don't forget—even if HIPAA doesn't apply to you, you should still use those standards as a framework to ensure appropriate privacy and security measures because the FTC and private actions can still apply to you. If you can show you've created a compliance program, it goes a long way toward demonstrating a good-faith effort.

I explain each of the seven elements here, briefly, and how a small organization or start-up can most reasonably meet those expectations.

1. Designated Compliance Officer

Clearly, it doesn't make sense for a small company to hire a full-time compliance officer. However, small companies do need to have someone designated, and that person will be responsible for developing and implementing the remainder of these elements.

There are a couple of ways to address the compliance officer requirement. The first way is to designate someone who is in a leadership role and add compliance to their stated responsibilities. The advantage, obviously, is that this person isn't costing the company any extra salary or benefits. The downside is that they may be swamped with their other responsibilities, depending on the scope of their role, and they also might not have expertise in some of the compliance requirements.

The second option is to outsource the role, either contracting with your own officer or sharing a resource with another organization if you have a partner organization and it makes sense for economies of scale. You could, for instance, share training materials or sessions.

One potential solution that combines both of these options is bringing in an expert to get your organization set up and trained and ensuring that you are addressing the various compliance risks, and then designating someone internally to manage the program going forward while keeping your trusted resource on the side for any incident or question that may arise.

Beyond having a designated person responsible for compliance, small organizations don't really need any additional program structure, such as a compliance committee. If your company grows or provides direct healthcare services, then you will want to explore the OIG's guidance for compliance program structure.

2. Training and Education

No matter what tools or services your organization provides, you need to implement certain training and education to ensure your staff are trained on the applicable laws and regulations. HIPAA, for one, is a focus area if you are in the health tech space and use or transmit patient data in any way. The Occupational Safety and Health Administration (OSHA) requires employee training for risk areas related to health and safety. You also need to train employees on your company policies—topics such as nonretaliation and anti-harassment, nondiscrimination, safety, and (depending on your services) fraud and abuse.

Your compliance training program can be relatively simple. You can find many free resources on government agency websites, such as OSHA's, that cover the agency's topics. If your organization provides direct healthcare services, take a look at the OIG compliance guidance documents for the risk areas you need to address. You can also find tools and resources through various partners, such as insurance companies or larger practices you're aligned with. Ask around and look online to get started. What some smaller organizations do is create a policy manual and then use that as their training tool: They have employees go through it and sign an attestation that they've read and agree to comply with the company policies.

My only caveat on creating a program: Don't just download canned policies and procedures and call it done. Do make sure you have what you need and that it addresses your specific risks and practice areas. At a minimum, have someone with compliance expertise review what you've pulled together to ensure you have covered the relevant risks and aren't missing anything or including things in a policy that your organization can't or won't be able to enact.

3. Standards of Conduct and Policies

Although larger organizations often create a code of conduct, smaller organizations typically have an employee manual and company policies. The employee manual contains employment-related policies, and these are important because labor law risks are prevalent in any organization. Make sure you have the manual either developed or reviewed by a labor attorney to ensure you are meeting your state and federal requirements around issues such as paid time off, medical leave, and timekeeping requirements.

Other policies are driven by the nature of your organization, but general categories include OSHA, HIPAA, fraud and abuse, employment practices (such as background checks, drug testing), and any other laws that apply. For instance, if you provide clinical laboratory services, you must meet Clinical Laboratory Improvement Amendments (CLIA) standards. Review the OIG compliance guidance documents for a list of compliance policies. Topics to consider include the following:

- Conflicts of interest
- Reporting and nonretaliation
- Record retention
- Sanctions/discipline standards (also required under HIPAA)
- Fraud and abuse
- Coding and billing

- Excluded providers/background checks/drug testing
- HIPAA policies
- Cybersecurity

4. Auditing and Monitoring

Auditing and monitoring are important components of a compliance program and also under HIPAA. Whether you provide direct patient care or merely an app that uses or transmits patient data, you need to review how you monitor the privacy and security of that tool.

Consider access management and physical security, which are always risk areas in almost any company or practice that uses confidential data.

The provision of patient care opens a whole different area of auditing, particularly if you bill government healthcare programs for the services. Are services properly ordered and documented? How is the accuracy of the bills ensured? Are you consistently following health and safety policies, such as infection control? Is medical necessity documented? These are general topics; depending on your practice area, you will have specific risks to address and monitor.

When it comes to this aspect of a compliance program, the best first step is to identify your potential risks. Risks differ by type of business and company or organizational structure. If you're not sure where to start, go through the laws, regulations, and cases in this book and review the OIG guidance documents. If you aren't doing any clinical documentation, coding, or billing, what about financial arrangements and referral arrangements? What are your marketing practices? How do you ensure the security of confidential data? Your specific risk areas are where you focus your policies, training, and education, and then, yes, auditing and monitoring to make sure the policies are being followed.

5. Corrective Actions

Once you have policies and procedures in place, everyone is trained, and an auditing or monitoring process has been implemented, you need to address the question of what to do when things go wrong.

People make mistakes, and not every failure to follow policy is intentional—in fact, most are not, and identifying those instances is an opportunity to retrain employees. The key here is to look at the whole issue and what went wrong to create a Corrective Action Plan. Too often, as a corrective action, a policy will be changed, but the employee, who was trained and should have known better, receives no discipline or retraining. What are all the factors that led to the problem? If it was a poorly drafted policy, then not only should the policy be changed but also staff should be retrained. Or perhaps a new law went into effect or regulatory requirements changed. When that happens, look at all the activities affected by the legislation and create a plan to systematically update all policies, procedures, and training.

There's one additional key point to note if you have anything to do with claims to government healthcare programs—overpayments. If you or your clients are reimbursed by a government program, you need to be aware that retaining any identified overpayment by a government healthcare program longer than 90 days is considered a violation of the False Claims Act. Managing overpayments should be part of your policies, education and training, auditing and monitoring, and corrective actions.

One of the most important general points to remember, however, is to document whatever corrective action you take. It might not "feel good" to put something in an employee's file, or maybe it seems like reporting that breach should be adequate, but, believe me, just like with clinical care, if it isn't documented, it didn't happen. You never know when the issue might come back to bite you—an employee that you terminate for cause tries to sue you, or the government does an audit and asks for all records pertaining to the issue. Not only that, but the manager who "talked to" that fired employee may no longer be with the organization. Always keep in mind that it's far better for you to find any problems and correct them yourself rather than have them come up in a government audit or a lawsuit.

6. Communications

Everyone talks about the importance of communications, and often people blame communication failures when things go wrong. Relative to compliance programs, however, *communications* refers primarily to avenues by which employees and others can report concerns. In most compliance guidance you will see reference to the "compliance hotline." Having an anonymous hotline for reporting concerns is definitely industry standard, whether that hotline is managed internally or by an outside vendor, and there are pluses and minuses for both approaches. If, however, you are a small start-up or small practice, setting up a hotline is likely overkill, and certainly paying for a vendor is an expense you don't want or need. But it does not eliminate the need for a way to allow employees, business partners, and even customers to report concerns to you.

Employees need to understand that you expect them to report concerns; it's part of their job. Most companies that you see in the headlines receiving heavy government fines didn't listen to their employees or business partners when something was wrong. Additionally, those fines will be less if you did listen and are already working on a solution. The government wants to see companies trying to do the right thing—mistakes are penalized at a much lower level than egregious conduct that is known and goes uncorrected.

Creating a reporting channel and process just makes sense, despite some of the irrational objections I've heard over the years. Why would you rather an employee call a lawyer or a government agency instead of handling their complaint internally? We hear a lot about whistleblowers, and this is how they are usually created: An organization isn't listening to its people. When an employee truly believes something is wrong and isn't being heard, it's not uncommon for them to leave their job and call someone outside to report the matter. And, yes, even that chronic complainer can be correct in what they are telling you and can't be ignored.

So, how do you address communications if you are a start-up or other small organization? With your internal team, it's important to establish a culture of no blame and to foster open, respectful communications. If you don't yet have a designated compliance person, probably the CEO or founder should clearly tell the team that they want to hear about anything going wrong and any anticipated problems. One-on-one communication should never be discouraged. You also want your business partners and clients to know that you want to hear from them. You can set up an email box and have a "let us know how we're doing" sort of blurb on your website and printed materials.

However you decide to do it, just be sure to consider all your stakeholders and how they communicate with your organization. Social media, printed or electronic bills—whatever it may be, you should make it easy for them to reach out to you with a concern. This isn't just a compliance issue; it's a customer satisfaction issue. Think about the big companies you've dealt with that make it impossible to talk to a person. That's not who you want to be. In addition, from a compliance perspective, you want to be able to show that you have an open-door policy and that honest communication is always appreciated and expected.

The other aspect of communications relates to the information being provided to employees. Your employees and anyone else working on your behalf should be kept informed of new laws, regulations, and enforcement activity as it relates to your business. Your designated compliance officer is responsible for those updates, but depending on the size of your organization, the CEO or someone else might routinely monitor the regulatory landscape. You can put this sort of information in an email, discuss it in a team meeting, or use any other internal communication mechanism; just be sure there is someone responsible for this because, with how fast the regulatory landscape is changing, today's information could be outdated by next week. Also, if you stay on top of proposed regulations, you can provide comments or, at a minimum, start thinking about how it impacts you and what to do so you're not scrambling at the last minute. Trust me, that's not a good place to be.

7. Disciplinary Standards and Exclusion Checking

I touched on this briefly earlier regarding corrective actions, but discipline is one aspect of a compliance program that the government calls out specifically. The main point here is that you want to have a standardized disciplinary process, even if it's very basic, so that you treat everyone consistently. If you are launching a small company, creating a disciplinary standard may not be at the top of your list, but if you have employees, at some point you will likely have to address discipline.

When the behavior at issue constitutes a compliance violation, discipline *must* be the same for every employee who has committed comparable violations. This may seem self-evident, but it's not always easy to do. For instance, you have a part-time worker who does scheduling for the clinical staff. You find out that she accessed medical records and looked up her neighbor, who was seen by one of your practitioners (this is why access controls are important!). This is a clear HIPAA violation, so you fire her (assuming she's been trained and you have policies in place about patient privacy). You hire a talented new young person to replace her, and all is well. Two months later, your best and brightest new physician does the same thing, snooping in his colleague's patients' records, which he has no reason to look at. He's also an employee. Does this give you heartburn? Probably so, especially if that physician brings a lot of value to your practice.

But take this a step further: Because this physician is so valuable, and it took months to recruit him, the executive team agrees to put him on a Corrective Action Plan. One of the nurses tells the fired scheduler about it. And perhaps that fired person was a member of a protected class, but your golden-boy doctor is not and neither is the new scheduler. You now have a problem, especially when that former employee calls her lawyer and every regulatory agency she can think of to allege discrimination. These are the types of scenarios you need to really understand and think through when writing your policies around discipline and, even more importantly, when those policies become pertinent in real life.

When it comes to discipline, you can reduce the likelihood of this occurrence if you conduct rigorous background and exclusion checks. The OIG expects healthcare organizations to conduct checks of the List of Excluded Individuals and Entities prior to contracting or hiring and routinely thereafter. The OIG provides a database you can easily search at exclusions.oig.hhs.gov, or you can hire a vendor to do it for you. This database includes those who are excluded from participation in government healthcare programs, and I can assure you, you don't want to hire or do business with anyone on that list because there are fines and penalties involved if the government catches you, particularly if that individual is providing patient care and billing for their services. The database is searchable or can be downloaded. This is one of the most important activities you can bake into your processes from the beginning, and it's simple to do.

One More Thing: Contracts and Vendors

Contracts and vendors is not an element of a compliance program, but it's a risk area that warrants being called out, particularly for tech companies and smaller practices that may not be aware of some of the compliance and regulatory risks related to business arrangements.

You can see in Chapter 6 on fraud and abuse how risks can arise if you improperly structure your financial arrangements, particularly when referrals for goods or services that are reimbursed by government healthcare programs are involved. This is a risk for any organization, not just the big guys.

Managing contracts and having certain core provisions in place are essential. If you read some of the cases throughout this book and online, for instance, on the HHS OIG and DOJ websites, you will see that financial arrangements are often at the center of the violations.

Here are a few core concepts you need to be aware of:

1. Always have your contracts in writing and keep them all in one repository. Missing contracts can create very large problems, and any "evergreen" agreements must be reviewed annually to ensure they are still appropriate. Document that review. This can also be a cost-saving measure because you can evaluate which services you are paying for but no longer need.

2. Have an objective process in place for selecting vendors. At a minimum, the leadership team should agree on the need for a certain type of vendor and can even decide who it might be as long as the person making the recommendation has no conflict of interest with the party. Ideally, you have a

process for selecting among several choices. Keep records of how you choose vendors, contractors, and business partners. Always ask and document any potential conflicts of interest. Anyone with a conflict should not vote. A conflict of interest exists if one of your team, or their immediate family member, has any type of financial arrangement with the vendor or some other loyalty that could come into play.

3. Make sure the contracts are fully executed (both parties have signed). Sounds obvious, but you would be surprised. Try enforcing a contract that someone never signed. Same thing goes for effective dates and signature dates. These sorts of details are why a contract database is strongly recommended.

4. All contracts should have language stating that the other party is not excluded from participation in any government healthcare programs, no such action is pending, and they will notify you if it does happen.

5. Vendors agree to follow all applicable laws, rules, and regulations, including but not limited to state and federal fraud and abuse laws, the Anti-Kickback Statute and Stark, the False Claims Act (state and federal), and HIPAA, as well as all privacy and security laws.

6. The agreed-on rate is for Fair Market Value and is not based on actual or anticipated volume or value of referrals.

7. If you are entering into any arrangement involving referrals for business or items that could be reimbursed by government healthcare programs, be careful to structure the arrangement in accordance with the Anti-Kickback Statute and, if physicians are involved, the Stark laws. It is a good idea to know an attorney who handles healthcare fraud and abuse so you can run potential arrangements by him or her.

Practice tip: Don't use your general business attorney for these sorts of questions. Arrangements and the analysis can be more complex than you realize and you want someone with solid expertise in healthcare fraud and abuse advising you. Your general attorney will likely try to help you, but you want an expert. It's money well spent.

Practice tip: Don't assume a service or product isn't reimbursed by government healthcare programs just because it isn't *directly* billed to the government payer. There are more than one way a service or supply can be considered "reimbursed" by government dollars. Think of things like government incentive programs, loans, cost reports, just to name a few examples.

Conclusion

This chapter is a very abbreviated outline of compliance program activities that you should implement if you are a healthcare provider of any type. Even if you don't provide healthcare services directly, chances are—if you're reading this book—you may well be a Business Associate of a provider or healthcare plan, in which case all of the above applies to you.

CHAPTER 9

Telehealth and Virtual Care: Setup and Operations

An important aspect to address in a discussion of telehealth and virtual care is the use of technology to improve the patient experience. Emerging technology and changing care models, such as value-based care, are designed to enhance care options and, ideally, optimize patient health. The various technologies outlined in this book are often important components of those new models, particularly when that care is largely provided in a virtual setting. Apps and wearables, for instance, can make a huge difference in managing chronic conditions and providing real-time information on the patient's condition. Care can be coordinated and managed through integrative technology that provides important notices to providers about their patients' status and condition.

In the past, it was up to the patient to recognize, for instance, that their blood glucose levels were not being well controlled or that they were having episodes of atrial fibrillation. Alternatively, it was the responsibility of the provider's office to follow up and check in with patients. Patients would be discharged after a procedure and go home without adequate medication reconciliation or follow-up care. But with the proliferation of various apps, devices, and wearables, patients and providers can now stay much better connected.

Whereas all of those are good things for patient care, this is still an evolving arena and the regulations are, in many instances, all over the map. Medical devices, as we've seen, are mostly regulated at the federal level, but the actual provision of care relies heavily on state laws. For that reason, this discussion of virtual care practices and telehealth is geared toward offering you an overview of the specific issues to address, rather than providing a "solution" for how to create such a practice.

With all of these services and applications of new technology, it is easy to see how complex the compliance world can become for a telehealth or virtual care provider. Not only do you have to be aware of and adhere to all the standards applicable to the specific technology you use, but you also have the same compliance responsibilities as other healthcare providers and, in some cases, more, because virtual services can cross state lines and trigger a wide range of state laws. In addition, the government, investors, patients, and other stakeholders will expect to see a virtual care provider implement a compliance program, just like any other healthcare practice does.

There are a number of action items to consider if you are developing a virtual practice or keeping a portion of your practice as telehealth. Keep in mind that each of these is a complex topic; here, I intend to provide a high-level road map of issues to consider and include in your planning. I'm dividing them into two parts: creation and setup of a telehealth organization, and operational issues.

Setting Up a Virtual Practice

A telehealth practice is largely governed by state-level laws, regulations, and licensure requirements that dictate what you can prescribe and how, whether you need to offer an initial in-person visit in order to provide telehealth services (or prescribe certain medications), and which services you can provide remotely, for example. Be sure to engage experienced legal counsel and other professionals to ensure your practice is meeting the vast array of requirements.

Legal Relationships and Duties

How are you going to structure the organization? Is it going to be a management services company (MSO) or an actual professional corporation? Where are you going to incorporate? You need to research the applicable laws and requirements for that state, particularly if you are going to be practicing medicine (as opposed to providing management services).

Is the organization going to be a subsidiary? What will the legal status be? As you consider these questions, consider the potential financial and regulatory and legal risks. Your insurance needs will also be impacted, so be sure to understand how the legal structure affects your risks and insurance rating.

In addition to your legal structure, you need to carefully consider how referral arrangements are structured. Although referrals are more of an operational issue, I include them here because those relationships also come into play when structuring an organization. Who is investing in the organization? Where do you expect to get referrals from? Be mindful of requirements under the Stark laws and Anti-Kickback Statute, not only with patient referrals but also when it comes to technology and durable medical equipment (DME) vendors. See Chapter 6 on fraud and abuse, as well as Chapter 7 on industry guidance, to get a good sense of where those risks reside.

Because this model of care is still evolving, it is hard to say how the government may decide to enforce these laws and what degree of scrutiny you could face. It is in your best interest to talk to a healthcare fraud and abuse attorney as you set up your various relationships and model.

Corporate Practice of Medicine

This is another state law consideration and relates to your business setup. *Corporate practice of medicine* means that the practice of medicine can be undertaken only by a professional corporation or other licensed entity. This can clearly affect how an organization is structured because states differ on who can own a company that practices medicine.

Knowledgeable legal counsel will help you identify the various state requirements where you plan to operate and how the profits are distributed so as not to run afoul of fee-splitting prohibitions (which, of course, also vary by state) and the Anti-Kickback Statute.

Location, Location, Location

Location is a huge issue in terms of where your providers operate and where patients reside. If Medicare, Medicaid, and other payers won't reimburse services, that's obviously a deal-breaker, so this is one of the most critical issues to get a handle on.

Licensure, as well, is impacted by location. Each state has different laws and regulations that address telehealth and the various specialties and their scope of license. This issue can get complicated very quickly in a virtual care practice that may be incorporated in one state with providers working from multiple different states and patients in different states altogether.

The impact of location is one of the key issues to analyze with your healthcare attorney early in the process so you can avoid costly mistakes down the road. More detail on the specific issues relating to licensure and reimbursement follows.

Licensing and Credentialing

Once you decide on your legal structure and location, questions of licensing are the next step. How many states will you need licensure in? What are the specific requirements in each state? Who needs licensure and in which states? How will licensure and credentialing information be maintained and kept current? And, keep in mind, depending on state laws, not only the clinician providing services but also the actual provider/owner may need state licensure.

According to HHS, health professionals must meet the licensure requirements of the state where they are located and be licensed or legally permitted to practice in the state where the patient is located. In response to the growing use of telehealth, many states are revisiting their licensure process to minimize barriers to access and ensure continuity of care while also preserving state regulatory oversight.

Licensure isn't just a one-time paperwork exercise either. Each license can cost between $75 and $800, and you have to consider the costs of various testing and ongoing education requirements for each state where you are licensed. I'm already visualizing the massive spreadsheet or database a provider organization needs to get started.

There is some relief, however. Some states have entered into a compact whereby they honor other states' licensure, and a number of states have endeavored to reduce the licensure burden by allowing for a registration process for telehealth services for out-of-state licensed providers.

According to HHS, under this telehealth registration pathway, there are certain state requirements and conditions. States can vary in how they oversee telehealth registration. Typically, providers must meet these terms:

- Must hold a current, valid, and unrestricted license in another state
- Must not be subject to any past disciplinary proceedings in any state where the provider holds a professional license
- Must maintain and provide evidence of professional liability insurance
- Must not open an office or offer in-person treatment in that state
- Must annually register and pay a fee with the appropriate state licensing board

Alternatively, multistate licensure compacts streamline the licensing process across states through one application while preserving state oversight of quality. Compacts, which are legal agreements among participating states, allow specific healthcare providers, such as physicians, nurses, psychologists, audiologists, and speech therapists, among others, to practice in states where they are not licensed as long as they hold a license in good standing in their home state.

Physicians are required to pay fees to participate in the compact, plus the cost of a license in any compact state where they wish to practice.[56]

The Interstate Medical Licensure Compact offers an option that includes all participating states (currently there are over 30 states participating). The fee is $700, plus whatever licensing fee applies by state. There is a website to check for fees and participation.[57] A telehealth or virtual health provider (or one investigating this option) should check this website as a source for good initial information regarding licensing across multiple states. There are, of course, specific requirements for any physician who desires to take advantage of the compact:

Any physician from a Compact state who meets the qualifications of the Compact is eligible for licensure in any other Compact state and responsible for obeying all statutory laws and administrative rules of the state.

To qualify for the Interstate Medical Licensure Compact participation, physicians must:

- Hold a full, unrestricted medical license in a Compact member state that can serve as a State of Principal License (SPL).
    - At least one of the following also must apply:
        - The physician's primary residence is in the SPL.
        - At least 25% of the physician's practice of medicine occurs in the SPL.
        - The physician is employed to practice medicine by a person, business or organization located in the SPL.
        - The physician uses the SPL as his or her state of residence for U.S. Federal Income Tax purposes.

(Note: Physicians must maintain their SPL status at all times. An SPL may be updated after a physician receives a letter of qualification to participate in the Compact.)

- Have graduated from an accredited medical school, or a school listed in the International Medical Education Directory
- Have successfully completed ACGME- or AOA-accredited graduate medical education
- Passed each component of the USMLE, COMLEX-USA, or equivalent predecessor exam accepted by the state medical board in no more than three attempts for each component. *—Please note: Passing the Canadian Licentiate of the Medical Council of Canada, or the LMCC, DOES NOT meet this requirement.*
- Hold a current specialty certification or time-unlimited certification by an ABMS [American Board of Medical Specialties] or AOABOS [American Osteopathic Association of Board of Specialty] board

In addition, physicians must:

- Not have any history of disciplinary actions toward their medical license
- Not have any criminal history
- Not have any history of controlled substance actions toward their medical license
- Not currently be under investigation

Each physician is responsible for making a self-determination of eligibility prior to applying to participate in the Compact, and they must confirm that they understand the Compact rules.[58]

There are a variety of state compacts for other types of clinicians, as well:

- Nurses
- Audiologists and speech pathologists
- Occupational therapists
- Physical therapists
- Psychologists
- Emergency medical services (EMS) personnel

A good resource on these various compacts, with links to learn which states are participating, can be found on the Health and Human Services website.[59] It's also important to note that behavioral health, although not part of any compacts, does have flexibility for cross-state services.

In certain situations, services can be provided without a license. In "The Appropriate Use of Telemedicine Technologies in the Practice of Medicine," the Federation of State Medical Boards outlines the following:

"There are a few instances, however, where certain exceptions may permit the practice of medicine across state lines without the need for licensure in the jurisdictions where the patient is located. These exceptions to licensure are only permissible for established medical problems or ongoing workups and care plans, or in cases of prospective patient screening for complex referrals. Should medical care be sought by the patient for a different medical diagnosis or condition, the physician must refer the patient to a physician licensed in the state where the patient is located or obtain a license to practice medicine in the state where the patient is located. Specifically, these exceptions are:

Consultations and Screenings
Physician-to-Physician Consultations The physician-to-physician consultation exception permits a consulting physician licensed in another state in which they are located to use telemedicine or other means to consult with a licensed practitioner who remains responsible for diagnosing and treating the patient in the state where the patient is located.

Prospective Patient Screening for Complex Referrals
- Physicians providing specialty assessments or consultations, such as at Centers for Excellence, are not required to obtain a license in the state where the patient is located in order to screen a patient for acceptance of a referral. The out-of-state physician may then provide care via telemedicine utilizing the physician-to-physician consultation exception above. If the out-of-state physician agrees to diagnosis, counsel, or treat the patient directly, the patient must travel to the state where the physician is licensed, or the physician must obtain a license to practice medicine in the state where the patient is located.

Episodic and Follow-Up Care for Established Patients
- *Episodic Follow-Up Care* A patient that is temporarily located outside the jurisdiction of a physician with which the patient has an established relationship may receive care via telemedicine technologies provided it is possible for the physician to gather sufficient clinical information during the evaluation to provide care that meets the accepted standard of care. If the patient is presenting with new medical

conditions, the physician may consider directing the patient to obtain local care. If the physician becomes aware that the patient's out of state location is no longer temporary, the physician should similarly develop a plan to transition care to a physician licensed in the state where the patient is located.

Physicians providing care under this exception should also be prepared to make referrals to a hospital or to a local specialist who can step in and assist, especially in cases of devolving medical or mental status.

Follow-up After Travel for Surgical/Medical Treatment Due to the unavailability, rarity or severity of a diagnosis or necessary treatment, a patient may choose to travel specifically to obtain specialty care at a medical center located in another state. In this situation, a significant portion of the diagnosis and treatment of the patient should occur in the physician's state of licensure, to include but not limited to, a surgical or procedural intervention. After the workup, procedure, or treatment is performed, the patient may return to their own state of residence and require additional follow-up care. When this follow-up can be effectively provided virtually, physicians should be allowed to utilize telemedicine without obtaining a license to practice in the state where the patient resides.

Physicians providing out-of-state care under this exception should ensure that their patients have backup plans to receive care locally if changes in their medical condition make that necessary.

Clinical Trials Physicians who work on clinical trials recruit patients based off certain criteria in hopes of increasing the likelihood of a successful and diverse clinical trial. When working on clinical trials that are enabled by telemedicine technologies, physicians should not be precluded from including patients that reside in a state where the physician does not have a license to practice medicine. Physicians providing out-of-state care under this exception should ensure that their patients have backup plans to receive care locally if changes in their medical condition make that necessary.[60]"

The Federation of State Medical Boards (fsmb.org) is also a good site where you can find resources related to credentialing, licensing, and other relevant information for physicians.

Accreditation

The Joint Commission has now launched an accreditation program specifically for telehealth practices. According to the Joint Commission's introductory statement:

> "The Telehealth Accreditation Program was developed for healthcare organizations that exclusively provide care, treatment and services via telehealth. Hospitals and other healthcare organizations that have written agreements in place to provide care, treatment and services via telehealth to another organization's patients have the option to apply for the new accreditation.
>
> The Telehealth Accreditation Program's requirements contain many of the standards similar to other Joint Commission accreditation programs, such as requirements for information management, leadership, medication management, patient identification, documentation, and credentialing and privileging. Requirements specific to the new accreditation program include:
>
> - Streamlined emergency management requirements to address providing care and clinical support remotely rather than in a physical building.
> - New standards for telehealth provider education and patient education about the use of telehealth platforms and devices.
> - New standards chapter focused on telehealth equipment, devices and connectivity.
>
> Additionally, the program's standards may be filtered based on the telehealth modality or service provided.[61]"

This new program was announced in April 2024 for a July 1, 2024, implementation date. Information on how to apply and additional details are available on the Joint Commission website, jointcommission.org.

Insurance

Telemedicine practitioners need to be aware of the various types of insurance policies that apply to their practice. There are malpractice policies for telehealth, and you should talk to your agent to get insurance in place before moving into this area of practice, or make sure that your existing policy includes such coverage.

In addition, have professional liability coverage as well as cybersecurity insurance. These are pretty standard policies to carry at this point. If you are going to be practicing in multiple states, be sure to verify that your plan covers you in all those locations. Also, depending on your practice, it might make sense to carry product liability insurance in the event of technology failures that could cause harm and where liability could reasonably fall to the provider.

Make sure you have an insurance agent who is experienced in telehealth and healthcare-technology-based practices to ensure that you are getting what you need but not more than is appropriate or reasonable for your organization.

Key Operational Issues for Virtual and Tele-health Practices

There are many decisions to make when getting up and running, but the following points must be considered.

HIPAA

We've discussed HIPAA's specific regulatory requirements elsewhere, but the other issue to consider is your organization's actual responsibilities. Are you a healthcare provider (Covered Entity) under the definition? Or a Business Associate (BA)?

Make sure you understand the basic requirements for information sharing and your organization's responsibilities. For instance, a healthcare provider doesn't need Business Associate Agreements if information sharing is for purely treatment purposes. But if you are structured as a management services company (MSO) and a BA, then a Business Associate Agreement is necessary for the actual providers to share patient health information with you. It's also important to understand that Business Associates have the same HIPAA responsibilities as Covered Entities, so the rules apply to you.

What if you are a Business Associate with subcontractors? You must ensure that any subcontractors who are using or accessing PHI are adhering to the same standards that you and the Covered Entity are. Most organizations use a Business Associate Agreement in such instances, but if you do so, be sure to carefully identify the parties because it can be confusing when neither party is a Covered Entity. If you have this situation, it might be worth your while to pay an attorney or consultant to help you make sure agreements are set up correctly. It can cause a lot of frustration, and potentially create costly errors, if these agreements aren't done right.

During the recent public health emergency, certain flexibilities were put in place in terms of enforcing HIPAA standards. Although the PHE has ended, the desire for telehealth has not. One of the areas of concern relates to the use of audio-only technology for telehealth services and how HIPAA is applied.

For actual landline telephone services, HIPAA does not apply, because the transmission of information is not electronic. However, the use of a landline for these services is becoming less and less common. HHS provides guidance for telehealth providers on this issue:

> "Traditional landlines are rapidly being replaced with electronic communication technologies such as Voice over Internet Protocol (VoIP) and mobile technologies that use electronic media, such as the Internet, intra- and extranets, cellular, and Wi-Fi. The HIPAA Security Rule applies when a covered entity uses such electronic communication technologies. Covered entities using telephone systems that transmit ePHI need to apply the HIPAA Security Rule safeguards to those technologies. Note that an individual receiving telehealth services may use any telephone system they choose and is not bound by the HIPAA Rules when doing so. In addition, a covered

entity is not responsible for the privacy or security of individuals' health information once it has been received by the individual's phone or other device.

For example, some current electronic technologies that covered entities use for remote communications that require compliance with the Security Rule may include:

- Communication applications (apps) on a smartphone or another computing device.
- VoIP technologies.
- Technologies that electronically record or transcribe a telehealth session.
- Messaging services that electronically store audio messages.

Potential risks and vulnerabilities to the confidentiality, integrity, and availability of ePHI when using such technologies need to be identified, assessed, and addressed as part of a covered entity's risk analysis and risk management processes, as required by the HIPAA Security Rule. A covered entity's risk analysis and risk management should include considerations of whether:

- There is a risk the transmission could be intercepted by an unauthorized third party.
- The remote communication technology (*e.g.*, mobile device, app) supports encrypted transmissions.
- There is a risk ePHI created or stored as a result of a telehealth session (*e.g.*, session recordings or transcripts) could be accessed by an unauthorized third party, and whether encryption is available to secure recordings or transcripts of created or stored telehealth sessions.
- Authentication is required to access the device or app where telehealth session ePHI may be stored.
- The device or app automatically terminates the session or locks after a period of inactivity.

As communication technologies (*e.g.*, networks, devices, apps) continue to evolve at a rapid pace, a robust inventory and asset management process can help covered entities identify such technologies and the information systems that use them, to help ensure an accurate and thorough risk analysis.[62]"

As I've noted throughout this chapter, one of the biggest challenges in providing a road map for telehealth involves the interplay between state and federal laws. Added to that is the fact that we are transitioning out of the COVID pandemic, which resulted in changed, negated, or relaxed rules or enforcement, and it can be a bit overwhelming to even know where to look first. One page that is a useful starting point for state healthcare laws is www.findlaw.com/state/health-care-laws.html. This page might not be totally up-to-date, but the links to the various laws and other pages will get you started.

Establishing the Patient–Provider Relationship

Start with the basics: What is your existing relationship with patients? This is an area where state laws and standards of care come into play, and you need to consider how you will establish the patient–provider relationship in the telehealth practice. You need to understand the requirements applicable to the specific services you are providing (behavioral health, for instance, as opposed to family medicine).

Can you take new patients without performing a physical examination? Think about how you intend to get a history and a physical. State laws differ on this point, with some states allowing an online survey to complete the patient's history and others requiring a more interactive interview. The American Medical Association has weighed in:

"The AMA [American Medical Association] believes that a valid patient-physician relationship must be established before the provision of telemedicine services, through: (i) A face-to-face examination, if a face-to-face encounter would otherwise be required in the provision of the same service not delivered via telemedicine; or (ii) A consultation with another physician who has an ongoing patient-physician relationship with the patient. The physician who has established a valid physician-patient relationship must agree to supervise the patient's care; or (iii) Meeting standards of establishing a patient-physician relationship included as part of evidence-based clinical practice guidelines on telemedicine developed by major medical specialty societies, such as those of radiology and pathology. Exceptions include on-call, cross coverage situations; emergency medical treatment; and other exceptions that become recognized as meeting or improving the standard of care.[63]"

Reimbursement

Reimbursement policy is one of the biggest changes that drove the movement toward virtual care. When HHS/CMS allowed reimbursement for certain telehealth services that were not previously covered (except under very limited circumstances), it opened the door. Not only that, but the convenience made virtual care a popular option with patients.

If it affects you, this is one topic you definitely need to monitor. I recommend visiting the CMS website (cms.gov) and signing up for email alerts to make sure you are immediately informed of pertinent developments.

Although there was a two-year extension, as discussed earlier, we still don't know what the permanent reimbursement structure will look like. At the time of this writing, well into 2024, reimbursement for a number of specific services has been extended through the end of 2024, and reimbursement is permanent for others: As of May 2024, the House Ways and Means Committee has drafted and passed the Preserving Telehealth, Hospital, and Ambulance Access Act, which would, among other provisions, extend telehealth coverage for two additional years (through the end of 2026) if it is makes it through the remainder of the legislative process.

Permanent Medicare Changes

- Federally Qualified Health Centers (FQHCs) and Rural Health Clinics (RHCs) can serve as distant site providers for behavioral/mental telehealth services.[64]
- Medicare patients can receive telehealth services for behavioral/mental healthcare in their home.

- There are no geographic restrictions on the originating site for behavioral/mental telehealth services.
- Behavioral/mental telehealth services can be delivered using audio-only communication platforms.
- Rural hospital emergency departments are accepted as originating sites.

Temporary Medicare Changes through December 31, 2024

- Federally Qualified Health Centers (FQHCs) and Rural Health Clinics (RHCs) can serve as distant site providers for non-behavioral/mental telehealth services.
- Medicare patients can receive telehealth services authorized in the Calendar Year 2023 Medicare Physician Fee Schedule in their home.[65]
- There are no geographic restrictions on originating sites for non-behavioral/mental telehealth services.
- Some non-behavioral/mental telehealth services can be delivered using audio-only communication platforms.
- An in-person visit within six months of an initial behavioral/mental telehealth service, and annually thereafter, is not required.
- Telehealth services can be provided by a physical therapist, occupational therapist, speech-language pathologist, or audiologist.[66]

We know with certainty that telehealth services with the following characteristics will continue to be covered by Medicare regardless of the extension:

- The beneficiary resides in a "qualifying" rural area (unless certain exceptions apply).
- The beneficiary is located at a "qualifying originating site."
- The services are provided by one of the ten allowed "distant site practitioners" who are allowed to furnish and be reimbursed for telehealth services by Medicare.

- The communication between the beneficiary and the telehealth provider are by way of an allowed interactive audio and video telecommunications system (with certain exceptions).
- The services for mental health and related disorders have been increased permanently for telehealth as well, so this is one arena where the requirements have been permanently loosened.

You can see by this list why the location factor is particularly important in telemedicine—not just for licensing reasons but also for reimbursement. I don't want to dwell too much on the "qualifying rural area" aspect because it currently isn't the requirement. It is important to note, however, that the current trend could be reversed unless Congress acts to make changes permanent, so we don't want to ignore it entirely.

A "qualifying rural geographic area" is a place in a rural healthcare professional shortage area outside of a metropolitan statistical area (MSA) or other rural census district outside of an MSA. Although there are detailed exceptions, it's safe to say that only facilities located outside of urban areas may qualify. If, after the two-year extension runs out, these standards are put back in place, I will update this book and provide more detail accordingly.

One of the other key requirements that is currently on hold has to do with the "qualifying originating site." This requirement stated that the patient has to be at one of the listed locations in order to receive telehealth services. Those locations were all various types of healthcare facilities, such as physician's offices, health clinics, and hospitals. Patients were allowed to receive telehealth services in their own homes only under very limited circumstances for specific conditions related to end-stage renal disease (ESRD), substance abuse treatment, or mental health disorders.

Right now, under the two-year extension, patients can receive many services in their homes. My opinion is that this practice will become a permanent benefit; people have become accustomed to this convenience, and it makes a lot of sense, particularly for mobility-challenged patients and those at risk for spreading illness or who are immune-compromised. I believe the pushback against changing this back would be tremendous.

Because Medicare rules can and do change regularly, to stay current I recommend you bookmark this site: List of Telehealth Services at https://www.cms.gov/medicare/coverage/telehealth/list-services.

Which providers can do telehealth services is another area that is expanded right now. For 2024, covered practitioners include the following:

- Physicians
- Nurse practitioners
- Physician assistants
- Nurse midwives
- Clinical nurse specialists
- Certified registered nurse anesthetists
- Clinical psychologists
- Clinical social workers
- Registered dietitians
- Nutrition professionals
- Qualified occupational therapists (OTs)
- Physical therapists (PTs)
- Speech-language pathologists (SLPs)
- Audiologists
- Mental health counselors and marriage and family therapists as distant site practitioners

Which services are covered and reimbursed by the various government and private payers? What is your relationship with accountable care organizations (ACOs) and payers? Payer acceptance of virtual services is rapidly increasing, but you need to know who will be partnering with and reimbursing your services. Then you have to put the proper compliance safeguards in place, including the applicable Business Associate Agreements, patient consents, contracts with payers and ACOs, and an ongoing plan for auditing and monitoring the billing of those services. And, of course, make sure you have a solid understanding of Medicare, Medicaid, and other government payer requirements in order to receive reimbursement.

How long does credentialing with the various payers take? It can be a lengthy process, particularly if the payer is newly accepting telehealth providers. If you are operating in multiple states, just know that the Medicaid payments and processes will differ across state lines.

Prescribing

Just like the licensure issue, many of the requirements related to prescribing medication are driven by state laws. The primary exception relates to the prescribing of controlled substances, although states issue their own regulations in this area as well.

Controlled substance prescribing has been addressed through the Ryan Haight Online Pharmacy Consumer Protection Act of 2008,[67] which requires that a practitioner prescribing a controlled substance through the internet conduct at least one in-person examination of the patient prior to prescribing the controlled substance in order for it to be a valid prescription. Although the Ryan Haight Act does not apply to telemedicine practices,[68] the telemedicine carve-out is very limited, allowing for only narrow circumstances where controlled substances can be prescribed without an in-person visit. Three conditions are required for this exception to apply:

- The patient is being treated by and is physically located in a hospital or clinic that is registered with the Drug Enforcement Administration (DEA) during the telemedicine encounter.
- The remote telemedicine provider is registered with the DEA in the state where the patient is physically located during the telemedicine encounter.
- The telemedicine physician interacts with the patient using a two-way, real-time interactive audio and video communications system during the telemedicine encounter.

The DEA waived this in-person requirement during the COVID PHE, allowing for the prescribing of controlled substances and buprenorphine (used to treat opioid use disorder) without a preceding in-person encounter. The DEA, on May 10, 2023, did address the question with a Temporary Rule, by extending the COVID flexible prescribing from May 11, 2023 (the day the PHE ended), until November 11, 2023, but also extending the option until November 11, 2024, in those instances where the patient–provider relationship was established prior to November 11, 2023, even if established in a telemedicine setting.

For substance abuse patients, on February 2, 2024, the Substance Abuse and Mental Health Services Administration, in conjunction with the Drug Enforcement Agency (DEA) issued a final rule that permanently allows patients to begin treatment with buprenorphine via telehealth. The rule also allows for increased flexibility related to methadone take-home doses, reducing the number of times patients must visit clinics. The new rule goes into effect October 2, 2024.[69]

Data Use and Sharing

Data use and sharing is a very significant piece of evaluating the setup of your telehealth organization. What data are you collecting, and from whom? Are you storing patient records from other providers? What patient consents are you obtaining for the use of their data? You need to be aware of how data will flow between you and payers, specifically, and be transparent about it. What electronic medical record (EMR) system are you using, and how does it interface with your other apps and tools? Who can access it?

In addition, how will you verify eligibility for a specific patient and payer? Who do you need to coordinate care with? What is the patient's relationship with the accountable care organization (ACO), and what is your relationship with that ACO? Who uses patient information for outreach? For marketing? As a provider, if you are, indeed, a healthcare provider and not an MSO, your records are medical records, so all the applicable regulations (state and federal) apply.

Are you using an app or other devices to store, schedule, or transmit patient data? If so, review the sections on those technologies in this book as well as the websites of agencies with oversight.

I strongly recommend that you map out your data flows and identify who is sending and receiving patient data and for what purpose. Identify who is a Business Associate under HIPAA and ensure the appropriate agreement is in place, but also review any other contractor that might have access to your data. For instance, other practitioners who also treat the patient are not considered Business Associates unless they are also performing services on your behalf, such as quality reviews. Other providers are Covered Entities, just as you are. That means they are also held to HIPAA standards, but you will want to obtain documented assurances that they have HIPAA-compliant processes in place. This can be through a data-sharing agreement or as part of a larger service agreement.

Informed Consent Processes

It's important to remember that even with telehealth visits, informed consent is still a requirement. Informed consent is yet another area where state laws may differ, but in general consider these practices:

- You can use your patient portal, if you have one, to share documents such as notices and consent forms with the patient. If the patient doesn't have access, the forms can be mailed. You can also generally obtain consent verbally, but make sure it's documented.
- Informed consent should be obtained prior to the first tele-health visit.
- Make sure the patient understands the technology that will be in use, is able to participate, and has no limitations that preclude use of the technology. For instance, if your service is audio only, is the patient hard of hearing? Does the patient have a language barrier (an interpreter may be needed)? Does the patient understand how to use the technology?
- If anyone else is going to be present during the visit, make sure the patient consents and document that consent.
- Provide the patient with an opportunity to ask questions.
- Always document any concerns or problems and be sure to address them before getting started with the visit.
- If you have patients who are minors, be sure you know your state's consent requirements. This is an important issue to understand not only for consent purposes but also in terms of privacy; if the patient is legally allowed to consent to their own care, for instance, for reproductive health services, they also have the right to restrict access to their records. This

can be a very sensitive issue, so be sure that your policies and procedures are consistent with the state laws.

Because of the variations in state laws, particularly if you are planning to practice in multiple states, have experienced legal counsel review your consent forms. Alternatively, be sure that the forms are developed by a reliable source.

The Center for Connected Health Policy website contains a wealth of information about telehealth laws and policies, and I recommend you check it out: cchpca.org. There you can find information on informed consent laws by state and reimbursement, licensure, and other topics. It is a page I have bookmarked.

Human Resources and Labor Laws

Human resources and labor laws apply as for any provider's office.

Are you going to hire employees or hire independent 1099 contractors? You need to conduct background checks, just as any other provider's office does, as well as exclusion checks (see Chapters 8 and 10 for additional details on that requirement). As a virtual provider, consider the scope of your background checks. In which state or states should background checks be run? In how many states does the person have a license? Do much more verification if your services will cross state lines.

I strongly recommend subcontracting the background checking and exclusion checking function. This will reduce your liability and give you assurance that all the appropriate requirements are being checked. Unless you are a very small practice, this is money well spent on risk reduction.

Case in Point: Fraud Alert!

On July 22, 2022, the OIG issued a Special Fraud Alert: "OIG Alerts Practitioners to Exercise Caution When Entering into Arrangements with Purported Telemedicine Companies." The genesis of this alert was a growing volume of fraud schemes involving telehealth. In these schemes, unscrupulous telemedicine companies paid physicians and other practitioners to generate medically unnecessary orders for durable medical equipment, genetic testing, wound care items, or prescription medications. These arrangements

---

implicate the Anti-Kickback Statute, the False Claims Act, and potentially other state and federal fraud and abuse laws.

Honest providers need to understand what these types of schemes look like in order to steer clear. The OIG is concerned with not only the costs to government healthcare programs but also the fact that medical decision-making is being undermined and could even cause patient harm. The OIG offers a list of indicators to alert you to a potentially unscrupulous arrangement:

- The telemedicine company has recruited the patient, whether through a call center, internet, or telemarketing company, often by advertising free or low out-of-pocket items or services.
- The clinician has minimal contact with the patient, thereby reducing the opportunity for actually assessing the medical necessity of the product or service they are being asked to prescribe.
- The practitioner is reimbursed on the basis of the volume of items or services ordered or prescribed, which may also be based on the number of medical records the practitioner reviews.
- The telemedicine company furnishes items and services only to federal healthcare program beneficiaries and does not accept insurance from other payers.
- The telemedicine company may claim to furnish items and services only to people who are not federal healthcare program beneficiaries, but may in fact bill those programs.
- The telemedicine company furnishes only one product or a single class of products, such as durable medical equipment, genetic testing, or diabetic supplies, thereby limiting the practitioner's options to a predetermined course of treatment.
- The telemedicine company does not expect or allow the practitioner to follow up with the "patients," nor does it provide the clinician with the necessary information to do so.

As this alert demonstrates, fraudsters are always ready to take advantage of any opportunity in the healthcare world. If you or one of your providers is approached with an opportunity that doesn't feel legitimate or has some of the qualities listed above, it's a good idea to steer clear or, at a minimum, get full information and check with an attorney or compliance expert before getting involved.

The OIG and the Department of Justice are dedicating many resources to this issue, but they also want to ensure that honest practitioners are not engaged in such schemes. They offer the following guidance for providers:

- Educate yourself and talk to your Federal health care program patients about the scope of telehealth services available to them through your office and other legitimate providers.
- Before providing telehealth to patients, verify that the furnishing of the telehealth service via a telecommunications system instead of through an in-person service is clinically appropriate for the service and the patient.
  - This verification may include checking with the patient that they have the necessary equipment to participate in tele-health visits.
- Ensure that you are assessing the medical necessity and reason-ableness of every item or service that you order or prescribe for a Federal health care program beneficiary.
- Make your patients aware of the types of communications they should expect to receive from your practice.
- Inform your Federal health care program patients that if they receive phone calls or other communications offering them durable medical equipment, genetic testing, diagnostic testing, diabetic supplies, prescription medications, or other health care items or services, they should consult you or another medical provider with whom they already have a provider-patient relationship to determine what, if any, items and services are needed to diagnose or treat their medical conditions.
  - You can expect that many of your Medicare patients are receiving unsolicited phone calls offering them "free" medical items and services.
- Be aware of phishing communications, including phone calls or faxes, stating that a clinical team determined that your patients

should receive certain items or services and requesting that you approve orders for various items and services.

- Report telehealth fraud to OIG's fraud hotline if you encounter it or if your Federal health care program patients inform you about it.[70]

The big takeaway from this Fraud Alert is to pay attention to the various arrangements you may enter. As a physician or other licensed practitioner, you may not immediately realize that an offer is suspect. Or maybe you're just setting up a practice. Not everyone has bad intentions, but mistakes can have bad outcomes nonetheless, so be scrupulous about your business relationships, and don't hesitate to get advice if you're not certain.

Conclusion

Building a telehealth practice involves many moving parts and multiple laws, regulations, and business requirements. If I were the one starting up this type of business, I would lean heavily on subject matter experts, attorneys, and consultants who know the most current options for insurance, licensure, reimbursement, and accreditation because, as I've said throughout this book, these are all evolving areas.

Your first job, however, is to review the resources provided here to orient yourself to the range of requirements and start planning on how to meet them or who to enlist for help. Also, keep an eye on the state compacts—I expect we will continue to see more states joining, and probably more specialties as well.

I believe that telehealth is only going to become more popular and a bigger piece of the healthcare landscape, so those who are already building these practices will be paving the road for others to follow.

CHAPTER 10

Occupational Safety and Health Administration

Who Needs to Read This: Healthcare providers, employers, and any healthcare or related organization with brick-and-mortar locations.

I almost didn't include this chapter. Occupational safety might not apply to your scenario and is not directly related to healthcare technology issues or rules. But I decided to keep it because I've encountered people in small practices and start-ups who weren't aware of basic workplace safety requirements.

Although this topic isn't the biggest risk area for many readers, if it helps just a few people, I'll be satisfied. If you have a purely remote workplace and aren't providing actual patient care services, this chapter likely isn't relevant for you. But such matters as hiring practices can be a safety issue, so you might want to skim this chapter even if you have only a few employees who work remotely. Even remote employees can create risk for the organization.

Workplace safety needs to be top of mind if you are providing any type of direct healthcare, even if all your workers are remote and you don't have an actual "workplace" where employees gather. The Occupational Safety and Health Administration (OSHA) develops and enforces the requirements intended to create safe working environments. These standards obviously affect healthcare practices, and OSHA develops requirements specific to healthcare in addition to standards that apply to all workplaces. The good news is that OSHA doesn't typically conduct random audits. The bad news is that workplace safety may encompass more than you initially imagine.

Occupational health and safety is another topic that could (and does) fill entire books, and it's a subject that I advise you to become well acquainted with, particularly if your employees provide healthcare in the field or you have an actual workplace where employees congregate or see patients.

In this chapter I highlight key safety risk areas under OSHA, emphasizing those that apply to healthcare. As mentioned, much of this discussion might not apply to your organization; it just depends on what services you provide and how. The best source for additional information, as well as access to the actual statutory language, is at the Department of Labor OSHA website.[71] Various states have their own workplace safety rules as well, which you can find online.

OSHA is a division of the US Department of Labor. The Occupational Safety and Health Act of 1970 (OSH Act) led to the development of the OSHA division as an administrative department. Unlike some laws, whose application varies depending on the employer's size, OSH Act covers *all* private employers in all states and the District of Columbia. OSH Act also applies to federal agencies unless they are specifically exempted because of coverage by another industry-specific agency. State and local government workers are not covered by OSH Act, although a number of states have enacted similar programs that are approved by OSHA.

In general, employers are obligated to provide a workplace without hazards that can result in death or serious harm to their employees. This includes specific requirements for employers to

- Identify and fix safety hazards and potential health threats
- Identify ways to improve working conditions, including by soliciting employee input
- Find ways to reduce risks posed by chemicals, such as by evaluating products for safer usage, improving ventilation, and so forth
- Create policies and procedures to promote workplace safety, and enforce them
- Develop policies and procedures to monitor work-related illnesses and injuries
- Create a workplace safety training program for employees

Operationally, although OSHA requirements are often assigned to the human resources departments in larger organizations, it is just one more hat for a start-up owner or small practice manager to wear. If you are providing healthcare services, OSHA requires healthcare practices to create and implement an OSHA compliance plan.

Just like the general compliance programs discussed elsewhere in this book, OSHA compliance programs include assessing risks, developing policies, correcting deficiencies, tracking problems, and training employees. There is also a requirement to have a designated OSHA or safety officer, and as with general compliance, this designated person is not expected to have a full-time role within the organization. The fundamental requirements of both OSHA and a compliance program are well aligned, which can lead to efficiencies in the tools you develop and how you roll them out to employees. With never enough hours in the day or money in the budget, efficiency is always paramount.

As you think about your OSHA compliance policies, be sure you know the core standards that apply to healthcare. Each standard has its own requirements, and probably the best way to meet them all is to create an OSHA binder or folder, similar to what you might be doing for HIPAA, that is accessible to all employees and contractors. Here are the topics to cover in the binder (if you only have employees working remotely, some of the following doesn't apply):

- Bloodborne Pathogen standard
- Hazard Communication standard
- Ionizing Radiation standard (if your services involve X-rays or radioactive substances)
- Exit Routes standard
- Electrical Safety standard
- Emergency Action Plan standard
- Fire Safety standard
- Medical First Aid standard
- Personal Protective Equipment standard

In addition to creating an OSHA folder to address these standards, you can take other specific steps to achieve compliance. As with HIPAA and other compliance topics, OSHA compliance can become a full-time occupation, especially if you have an actual workplace with employees on-site, but also when you consider the risks that need to be addressed with remote employees who enter patient homes.

Although I would never discourage anyone from dedicating their efforts to compliance, apply a reasonableness and feasibility standard to your efforts, ideally one that is based on an evaluation of risk. Let's look at a couple of key healthcare risk areas as well as some general safety risk areas that come up frequently. Note that these are for healthcare generally, not specific to mobile health services or remote employees.

Common Challenges and Violations

OSHA inspections do happen, and infractions, along with necessary steps to remediate, are documented. Although the chances of experiencing a random OSHA inspection are not huge (and virtually nonexistent if everyone in your company works remotely), you don't want a complaint or media coverage related to a safety issue that could have been prevented. Plus, most importantly, you don't want anyone to get hurt!

The top 10 list of healthcare risk issues differs from that of the general workplace. I have reviewed both and identified what I believe are the areas where a start-up or small healthcare provider should focus its efforts:

- Bloodborne pathogens
- Hazard communications
- Human behavior and hiring practices

Bloodborne Pathogens

When I talk to healthcare practitioners about risk areas where they want better tools and understanding, bloodborne pathogens is often at the top of the list. Although this may be an instinctive concern by administrators, it is justified by the frequency of citations in this area of risk. And if you are providing healthcare services that may involve needlesticks in patient homes, this is a big area for you.

As the name suggests, the OSHA Bloodborne Pathogens Standard requires employers to develop and implement an Exposure Control Plan intended to prevent or reduce exposure to bloodborne pathogens. Part of that plan includes identifying the various jobs and tasks that could result in employee exposure.

Another key activity, which derives from the Needlestick Safety and Prevention Act of 2000, is to implement an ongoing process for reviewing and updating devices and techniques to ensure that the safest and most current practices are in place. Employees whose jobs involve these potential hazards need to be engaged to provide this input because they not only have the biggest vested interest but also are probably the most up-to-date on emerging industry standards. If you have nurses or phlebotomists, these are the people to ask.

The following activities are core components of your Exposure Control Plan. The plan needs to be documented.

a. **Exposure determination.** Identify and list all job classifications/titles, tasks, and activities with potential to expose employees to bloodborne pathogens.

b. **Employee input on new technology and devices.** Employers need to engage those employees who are at risk for exposure to bloodborne pathogens on an ongoing basis to identify new technologies, better techniques, best practices, and emerging practices that could improve safety in their roles and related activities. This input should be documented and evaluated, with an implementation plan where warranted.

c **Universal precautions.** Employees must be trained to assume that any materials are contaminated with bloodborne pathogens or other hazardous infectious materials and to take the maximum safety precautions accordingly.

d. **Engineering and work practice controls.** Proper control of sharps and sharps disposal containers, needleless devices, and hand hygiene need to be exercised consistently, and all healthcare workers who potentially could be exposed need to be consulted, engaged, and thoroughly trained in the appropriate precautions to prevent exposure. In addition, such employees also need to be engaged in evaluating best practices, techniques, and products to prevent any avoidable exposure.

e. **Housekeeping.** Appropriate procedures need to be developed, implemented, and followed to ensure the appropriate decontamination and safe disposal of regulated waste.

f. **Personal protective equipment (PPE).** PPE includes items such as goggles, face shields, gloves, gowns, and aprons. Employers need to require the use of PPE as part of the exposure prevention activities and must provide PPE to employees at no cost to employees. This is even more critical now, with COVID- and infection-control efforts being paramount.

g. **Hepatitis B vaccination.** Employers must provide the option of hepatitis B vaccination, at no cost to employees, within 10 days of assigning an employee to a potential risk area. Any employee who declines the vaccine must sign a form declining the vaccination, and the employer needs to retain that record.

h. **Exposure/incident reporting.** Employees must report exposure incidents right away, and the employer must have a process in place to immediately address the potential exposure, including an immediate and confidential medical evaluation and follow-up, at no cost to the employee. Employers need to use these incidents to track and investigate safety risks and to develop corrective actions where appropriate. Records of all exposures and incidents need to be maintained, along with the steps taken in response, both for the individual employee and within the organization, to the extent the incident was caused by a process or control failure.

As with all compliance-related activities, documentation is key. Clinical personnel are frequently trained on the concept of "if it isn't documented, it didn't happen." This is absolute with respect to safety practices. Ongoing risk assessments, procedure and technology revisions, training, and incidents with corrective actions all need to be documented thoroughly.

Hazard Communications

The OSHA Hazard Communication Standard refers broadly to the right of employees to know of hazards that exist in the workplace and, more specifically, of chemical hazards that may expose them to harm in the workplace. Under this standard, employers are required to make information available to employees informing them of these potential risks, thus meeting the requirement that employees have the "right to understand" the hazards.

The Hazard Communication Standard, now known as HazCom 2012, is aligned with the United Nations Globally Harmonized System of Classification and Labelling of Chemicals. It contains several categories of key requirements:

- Hazardous material classification
- Standards for labeling hazardous products and materials
- Safety Data Sheets (SDS, formerly MSDS)
- Employee training and information

You won't be surprised to learn that OSHA requires a designated employee lead the efforts for managing the Hazard Communication Standard program. This individual can assume responsibility for all the related activities or can assign them but is ultimately responsible for making sure the standards are being met.

The Hazard Communication coordinator must put together a written program to document how the standards will be met and to ensure that employees are equipped with the necessary information on the various chemicals they could be exposed to in their workplace. In addition to identifying the specific products and materials potentially present, the program also outlines the appropriate measures for employees to take to protect themselves.

One key measure to protect employees from exposure to hazardous chemicals is, not surprisingly, a process for clearly labeling all such chemicals. OSHA requires a number of specific elements be on the product labels:

a. **Product identifier,** which includes the chemical's name and the code or batch number designated by the manufacturer/importer/distributor that matches the identifier found on section 1 of the Safety Data Sheet for that product/chemical.
b. A **signal word** that identifies the degree of severity of the hazard, such as "Danger" or "Warning."
c. A **hazard statement** that explains the nature of the danger, such as "Harmful If Swallowed" or "Highly Flammable."
d. **Pictograms** in conjunction with the signal word and hazard statement, for instance, a representation of a fire for flammable substances.
e. **Precautionary statements** that explain how to minimize the risks posed by the chemical. There are several categories, and the statements must match those given on the Safety Data Sheet for the corresponding product. The categories of statements are as follows:
   - Preventative (what personal protective equipment should be worn, etc.)
   - Response (what to do in the event of an incident, such as what to use to extinguish a fire)
   - Storage ("Store in cool dry location," for instance)
   - Disposal (in accordance with regulations or manufacturer instructions)
f. **Manufacturer/supplier information,** including the emergency phone number, which is vital to ensure that contact can be made quickly in the event of an emergency. This information needs to be kept current, both by the manufacturer and by the Hazard Communication coordinator, who must routinely compare the label to manufacturer information to capture any updates.

Safety Data Sheets need to be maintained for every hazardous chemical present in your practice setting. These SDSs are supposed to be provided by the manufacturer or supplier, including updates to any SDS upon updates to the information. Unlike retention periods for many documents, your practice should not keep any SDS sheets for products no longer in use or on-site at your practice. You also don't need to maintain these sheets for nonhazardous chemicals, such as common cleaning supplies.

The SDS should always follow the format and include the data elements as identified in HazCom 2012:

a. Identification
b. Hazard identification
c. Composition/ingredient information
d. First aid measures
e. Firefighting measures
f. Accidental release measures
g. Handling and storage
h. Exposure control/personal protection
i. Physical and chemical properties
j. Stability and reactivity
k. Toxicological information
l. Ecological information
m. Disposal considerations
n. Transport information
o. Regulatory information
p. Other information

Documentation is critically important in this arena, because of the risk potential. Make sure that you have an SDS for all applicable products and that they are available to staff under any circumstances. For instance, it's fine to make them available electronically, but that should not be the only option in case of a power outage or technology issue.

In addition to making certain you have all the data sheets, employees must be trained on these requirements and how to use the safety data on the labels and SDSs. Employees also need to be trained on risks and precautions related to the specific chemicals that are present at the practice and that they may come into contact with. This training should occur for new employees and annually. And, as I keep saying, make sure that the training is documented, including the content and the attendance or other report that tracks employee participation.

OSHA has a general duty clause that basically encompasses all those potential hazards and risks that an employer knew (or should have known) about that can foreseeably cause harm to workers. It's important to know that this category can include a broad range of risks, from overloaded electrical outlets to an obviously drug-abusing employee. Fire and building codes are a common area of concern in this category, but many others can come into play.

This is one reason that you need to pay attention to complaints and reports from employees and others. Once they tell you or report it, you are on notice; and, in addition to any other potential avenues for reporting externally, an OSHA claim may be raised and trigger a review.

Human Behavior and Hiring Practices

Some of the things that may not immediately come to mind with respect to OSHA relate to human behavior as a risk.

Other state and federal laws may apply, depending on the facts and issues, but I'm just pointing these out so you can keep them in mind. The "human factor risks" that you should address in policies and training include discrimination, anti-harassment, and nonretaliation and workplace violence.

Discrimination, Anti-harassment, and Nonretaliation

One frequent area of confusion is thinking that an anti-harassment and nondiscrimination policy and training address the issue of nonretaliation. In a smaller company or practice, you don't need separate policies, but it's important to understand the distinction and address both types of behavior in your policies and training.

In general, *harassment* is mistreatment based on membership in a protected class, whereas *retaliation* is adverse treatment based on participation in a protected activity, such as reporting violations of law.

Discrimination, harassment, and retaliation are all illegal. If you provide training on the necessary nondiscrimination and anti-harassment laws and policies but don't ensure that everyone understands what retaliation looks like, you can end up with lawsuits or visits from enforcement agencies.

OSHA has some good guidance about retaliation,[72] and you can find great information on harassment on the Equal Employment Opportunity website.[73] Nonretaliation is also a core topic in compliance programs, so I would strongly recommend drafting a nonretaliation policy and guidance with these standards in mind.

Workplace Violence

When it comes to healthcare and workplace safety, the topic of workplace violence and active shooters is most frequently associated with hospitals. This is not surprising, given the diverse populations hospitals serve: patients with a full range of mental and physical ailments. An emergency department can be a beacon for a behavioral health patient in crisis, a drug-addicted person desperate for medication, or even someone with a physical problem that has become so severe it's become a psychiatric issue. With all that said, any workplace accessible to the public can also be affected.

Although patients with mental health problems or other issues are the common concern in healthcare, other potential workplace violence scenarios are also possibilities, such as an angry ex-husband, a teenage child in the midst of a psychotic episode, the terminated employee, a scorned lover . . . you see the possibilities, and they are, unfortunately, proven as risks in the news every day.

A variety of policies and training for workplace violence is available. OSHA requires employers to have a workplace violence plan in place, and employees need to be trained not only on how to respond to incidents but also on how to recognize possible warning signs.

Of course, there is no total solution to workplace violence. As long as you have people, there is a chance of someone going over the edge, and it's usually not expected (otherwise we, in healthcare, would have done something to help prevent it!). The best thing we can do is to identify the potential scenarios and create policies and procedures to train our staff. There are some steps to consider, such as security cameras, minimizing cash on hand, and instituting solid security protocols.

Disruptive behavior is an issue that can affect patient care and the safety of the workplace, whether employees or providers act disruptively toward patients or fellow employees and providers. Disruptive behavior has been a big enough issue in the hospital setting that the Joint Commission made it a required element to be addressed with policies and training.

Specifically, be sure to include a couple of key elements in your policy. One critical piece is defining the behavior you consider disruptive. You may already be certain of ongoing patterns that should be addressed, but definitely include others. Your list of disruptive behaviors can be rather broad, well beyond verbal abuse and yelling. Think about the following:

- Making demeaning or insulting, unconstructive comments or criticizing
- Refusing to cooperate with reasonable work requests
- Deliberately obstructing, ostracizing, or creating difficulties for another employee
- Making hostile, racially insensitive, or sexually inappropriate jokes or comments
- Arguing with or complaining to colleagues in the presence of patients or visitors
- Making physical outbursts, such as slamming a door or throwing things
- Yelling or cursing

In addition to listing the behaviors, you also need to clarify how the behaviors will be addressed, and this needs to include the behavior of contractors, employees, physicians/clinicians, students, and anyone else who is working on your behalf. You may decide that an employee will get one written warning if an investigation confirms the behavior, but the next incident will result in a more severe sanction or termination.

The tricky part is training everyone on the disruptive behavior policy, making it clear this is a very real expectation, and then enforcing it. Nobody enjoys disciplining for behavior; it feels very personal. But bad behavior can put your workplace at risk to varying degrees depending on the nature of the infraction. Unfortunately, this is an area where issues can't be allowed to escalate.

In addition, you need to consider disruptive behavior when it comes from patients or their families. What will your policy be for providers who go into patients' homes and are verbally abused or harassed? This is an issue to think through when drafting consents or other documents that patients receive when they sign up for services, and, of course, training for staff who could be impacted.

You can address behavior in the code of conduct, should you choose to develop one. That's another good place for this topic. The employee handbook, as well, should include some reference to core requirements and expectations on behavior. Another option is to include it in your anti-harassment policy, which you definitely need to have.

The anti-harassment policy prohibits any harassment by or against any employee, contractor, physician, patient, visitor, student, or other person. This policy must specify harassment based on race, national origin, gender, sexual orientation, and disabilities. No retaliation is allowed for good faith reporting of harassment, either. This policy is often part of the nondiscrimination policy; many examples are available online. Start with the Equal Employment Opportunity Commission (EEOC at www.eeoc.com) or the Office of Civil Rights (www.hhs.ocr.gov).

Hiring Practices Can Also Create a Safe Workplace

Although hiring practices are more in the human resources realm, I mention here some aspects of the hiring process and the human behavior risk factors that affect workplace safety. After all, if we hire a person with certain psychiatric problems, a history of behavior or drug issues, or previous criminal legal trouble, we are definitely increasing the probability of something bad happening in our organization. Although there are no guarantees in life, some risks can be minimized through consistent and effective employee and contractor screening.

Some of these hiring practices may seem obvious, but I've encountered instances when all precautions were neglected, namely:

- Background checks
- Exclusion checks
- Drug tests
- Contracts for temporary staff

177

Background Checks

State laws govern background checks, but even if you aren't required to verify the (lack of) criminal background of your employees, you should certainly do it. In addition, if an employee has recently moved from another state, you should check that person's background. In most states this means a process administered by the state patrol. Some states require checks through the Federal Bureau of Investigation (FBI) under certain circumstances or for nonlicensed direct care workers. You will find a lot of variation across states, with requirements differing by types of checks required and which workers should be checked.

Why would anyone not do criminal background checks? For one thing, they can take time, and often an employee is needed right away. But skipping a background check is clearly risky, especially if you are hiring someone who provides direct patient care. Imagine hiring a nursing assistant and putting that person to work where they engage in some form of sexual abuse of a patient, then you discover they had a record of such abuse in the state they just moved from. Think of the potential harm to the patient as well as the resulting lawsuits and reports to government oversight agencies. Imagine, too, what the headlines in the local paper would have to say about that.

Background checks also cost money and can be a hassle. Some states require fingerprints on specific forms, for instance. If a state doesn't require background checks, and the checks are cumbersome, some practices don't do them.

Or they employ an inconsistent process because they are small, and hiring is infrequent.

You probably can guess what my advice is in this area: Establish a policy and procedure to ensure that all employees undergo a criminal background check before hiring, and be particularly diligent with any employees who provide direct patient care or who have responsibility for your billing or patient health records. Those are your big risk areas, where you don't want any preventable lapses. One area where you might show some leniency is for licensed providers if their credentialing with the licensing board is relatively recent, depending on the rigor of your state's background checks for licensure.

Applicants need to consent to the background checks, so consult your state requirements regarding the specific forms needed as you create your background check process.

Exclusion Checks

Exclusion checking is an issue that many people are unfamiliar with unless they've worked in compliance or HR departments in larger healthcare organizations. *Excluded individuals* and *excluded entities* are people or organizations that are excluded from participating in government healthcare programs. There are a variety of reasons for the exclusion: healthcare fraud, abuse, or in some cases even defaulting on student loans.

Most states have some form of exclusion or "sanction" listing, usually posted through the state's health department. The federal database is administered by the Health and Human Services Office of the Inspector General (OIG) and is called the List of Excluded Individuals and Entities (LEIE).[74] You can easily search the website for a company's or potential employee's name.

The bottom line regarding excluded individuals and entities is that you don't want to hire or contract with them; neither do you want to provide services based on an order from an excluded individual. The amount of the fines your practice can be subjected to can be astronomical, so it's definitely not worth the risk.

The OIG recommends checking all employees and contractors prior to entering a relationship with them and then checking monthly thereafter. In addition, the OIG has advised Medicaid agencies to require their providers conduct exclusion checks, so you may find yourself obligated by contract with a payer to implement a policy and procedure to conduct these checks up front and monthly. For a very small organization, I would recommend establishing a regular process that seems reasonable to your size. Obviously, if you have only three employees at the start, and don't add anyone for six months, you are unlikely to have a problem (but you never know!).

In addition to your own checking, include on your employment applications a question about whether the applicant has ever been excluded from participation in a government healthcare program. If yes, they need to explain where, when, and the facts around the exclusion. If the individual is still excluded, you won't be able to hire them. Any practice with an excluded individual working for them can be subject to heavy civil monetary penalties, so it definitely isn't worth it.

Licensed healthcare providers go through a background check process as part of their credentialing, which gives you some assurance about individuals licensed in your state. Be very sure, however, to verify licensure. Also, sad to say, people lie on applications and résumés, so verify all of an applicant's credentials.

Another obvious requirement is to have an actual application form. It may surprise you to learn that some practices don't really have one. You need an application so that you are able to inquire about these types of issues—criminal history, government healthcare program exclusion, and so forth. It will protect you in the event you do discover any misrepresentation because you can easily prove it.

Drug Tests

Certain employers must comply with specific legal requirements to maintain a drug-free workplace. The requirements apply to federal employers but also any organization that receives a federal contract of $100,000 or more or any organization receiving a federal grant of any size. See guidelines on the Drug-Free Workplace Act of 1988 for a discussion of those requirements posted on the Substance Abuse and Mental Health Services Administration website.[75] Your practice may be subject to additional requirements depending on your state, insurance carriers, or accreditation agencies, as well.

Most notably, though, is the fact that drug testing as a condition for employment is not required under federal law. It may be required through one of the other channels just mentioned, but you need to carefully consider this issue, especially if you provide direct care services or keep an inventory of high-risk drugs on-site, where an employee who is addicted or who abuses drugs could be tempted to divert those medications. This is another one of those issues most people don't often think about from an OSHA perspective, but complaints have been filed against providers who didn't conduct either preemployment or random drug tests. I don't think I need to explain how an employee who abuses drugs can create an unsafe workplace!

My preference is to conduct preemployment drug tests once an offer has been made, and let employees know that random drug tests or tests for cause may also be performed. I don't see any legitimate reason for not drug testing, and drug abuse is an avoidable risk, to some extent.

If you have a relationship with an employment law or labor law attorney, double-check with them after you have done your own research and set up a process for managing this issue. Be certain, as well, to get guidance on your policy if you are located in a state that allows the use of marijuana, either for medical purposes or recreational.

Contracted Staff Contracts

Another area often overlooked is how OSHA and general compliance and HR requirements relate to contracted staff and students. The issues typically are about training these employees on compliance, HIPAA, and OSHA safety standards and screening these individuals for employment.

Bringing contracted workers into compliance in the practice should be pretty simple: Review your agreements with employment agencies, schools, and other organizations that provide healthcare workers to your practice. Also check agreements with subcontractors and for in-office services provided by other companies, such as clinical labs that provide an on-site phlebotomist. Make sure that you've identified everyone who could meet the legal and the practice's requirements for health and safety compliance and that either your agreements state the supplying agencies will address compliance issues (and provide documentation) or you are prepared to manage compliance.

Make sure agencies or schools have conducted background checks on contract workers and students that are consistent with your needs and expectations, including criminal background checks and checks against the Health and Human Services List of Excluded Individuals and Entities. This list, discussed previously, contains names of individuals and organizations that are excluded from participation in government healthcare programs. Most states also have a comparable list, and many managed care contracts require checking the lists monthly. How you handle background and exclusion checking can vary, depending on the specific role and duration of an individual's engagement with your practice. At the least, you want assurances that criminal background checks and exclusion checks have been completed. Otherwise, be prepared to do them yourself. These are nonnegotiable requirements in healthcare, as you know. The only question is who is doing them, and then ensuring that organization provides documentation.

Education and training are other key issues for temporary and contracted staff and students. Make sure all individuals working in your practice have had basic OSHA, HIPAA Privacy and Security, and compliance training. The level of effort you expend ensuring contracted workers are given compliance training will vary, depending on the duration of their time with you. If an employment agency sends staff who are typically there for months, for instance, to cover short-term disability or maternity leaves, then review the material they've been trained on to verify its adequacy or perhaps simply require the employees to take your training. You can put longer-term contracted staff through new employee orientation and have them review and sign off on the code of conduct if you have one. You have some degree of flexibility here but should establish your standards for these types of employees on the basis of their role and length of engagement, and then follow these standards consistently.

Also, it's important to keep in mind your organization's health and safety requirements for healthcare workers, such as tuberculosis testing and flu shots. Do you require drug testing? For workers who are on-site only for short periods of time, these matters can be difficult to handle in a timely way, but the organization or school you are working with should already have policies in place, especially for items required by law.

One More Thing—Lawsuits

In healthcare, when a patient brings a malpractice case the outcome often depends on the standards of care. Which standards and protocols were in place guiding the particular service in question, and were those followed? Often, people forget, or perhaps don't realize, that the same thing applies in other aspects of healthcare.

The laws, regulations, Fraud Alerts, and cases cited throughout this book are examples of what is now the standard of care as it relates to privacy, security, and other risk areas. Although it's true, as many pointed out in the past, that there is no "private right of action" under HIPAA doesn't mean that only the regulators can penalize you for a failure to protect the privacy and security of patient data. HIPAA is the standard of care, along with the FTC guidance and all the other alphabet-soup guidance documents you can find.

If you aren't convinced, check out this final Case in Point:

Case in Point: Perry Johnson & Associates

Perry Johnson & Associates is a company that provides medical transcription services to many large healthcare providers. In terms of HIPAA, it is a Business Associate.

During the period of March through May 2023, PJ&A was hacked, exposing millions of multiple clients' patients' Protected Health Information, including names, dates of birth, details of healthcare services received, and even Social Security numbers. The total number of affected patients was estimated at around nine million, making this the sixth-largest breach ever. Notifications were sent out November 10, 2023.

Because of the size of the breach—more than 500 people impacted—it was reported to Health and Human Services, as required, which will do its own investigation.

In the meantime, more than two dozen lawsuits have been filed. Those lawsuits name not only PJ&A but also the providers who engaged the company (the Covered Entities). Some, if not all, are class action lawsuits. Some of the healthcare organizations affected include Northwell Health, Salem Regional Medical Center, Mercy Medical Center, and Crouse Health.[76]

What are the actual causes of action in the Case in Point?

- Negligence
- Negligence per se (citing FTC Act and elements of unfair or deceptive practices)
- Breach of contract
- Breach of third-party beneficiary contract (data security was an element of the contract between the parties/defendants)

This case is a wonderful (although not at all pleasant) example for Business Associates, Covered Entities, and other healthcare companies. What are some of the facts that make this case so compelling?

- PJ&A waited six months to notify consumers of the breach. Although the company claimed it rectified its security issues immediately upon discovery (May 2), the affected individuals had no knowledge of the matter and could not take steps to monitor their own credit or take other actions.
- The notice didn't give details on how the breach happened, how many individuals were affected, or other key information that is supposed to be included in breach notifications.
- For the health systems/facilities, it isn't clear how much effort they made in verifying the security measures in place with their Business Associates. It's likely, however, that the contracts had standard HIPAA language holding the vendor to HIPAA and other applicable data security standards. The due diligence in selecting the vendor, however, will be called into question during the course of these lawsuits.
- The complaint provided very detailed information about the standards promulgated by not only HIPAA but also the FTC, at length, and other agencies. These are the standards that were violated, leading to claims of negligence (breach of duty of reasonable care), unfair/deceptive trade practices, and so forth.
- The sheer volume of people impacted—nine million.

So, what's the lesson here? Well, there are multiple points, but the main idea is that violations of the laws and regulations can come back to bite you, even if the regulators aren't the ones who raise the issue. And rest assured, regulators won't be far behind regardless of who reported the issue, at least for the larger cases with mandatory reporting requirements.

The other point relates to Business Associates: they are held to the same HIPAA standards as Covered Entities, but a failure by a Business Associate can harm many more individuals if they have patient information from multiple clients. The damage increases exponentially. Covered Entities need to conduct solid due diligence when contracting with vendors who will use, transmit, or disclose health information.

What does that due diligence look like? Have someone in the organization who understands your compliance and HIPAA requirements review the vendor's policies and procedures to see what it has in place. Have your privacy or security officer talk to the vendor's to get information on how the vendor program is structured, what training is provided to employees, and how it monitors the use and access of protected data. Ask the vendor about its Security Risk Assessment and the resulting workplan. Any company that can't confidently answer these basic questions might not be a good vendor to partner with.

Conclusion

Workplace safety covers a broad range of risk areas. Be aware that many states have their own version of OSHA and may include additional or more rigorous requirements.

Also, OSHA does not inspect employees' home offices or worksites, so remote employees do not have to worry about OSHA requirements absent some very unusual circumstances.

Final Thoughts

Healthcare technology was booming before COVID; now it's booming on a whole other level, and the number of start-ups and new device applications and approvals is staggering. Artificial intelligence adds another layer of complexity to this new world, not only technologically but also legally and morally. Are we moving too fast? And can humans keep up with the machines we've created? These are fascinating times we live in, and being involved in healthcare is perhaps the most exciting place to be right now.

This book has been my most challenging project to date. The laws, cases, and guidance are changing so fast you can almost watch it happen in real time. For that reason, I included a lot of links, resources where you can go to get the latest information.

Also, one final disclaimer: Nearly every government agency out there is looking into AI and other technological changes. This book addresses those that are the more active for healthcare technology, but you will see opinions, guidance, and probably new laws and regulations continue to emerge. Your best bet is to check out the resources I've identified here and bookmark them or sign up for email alerts.

I am staying on top of developments, too, so follow me on LinkedIn (linkedin.com/in/susanwalbergjd) or at my website to stay informed: susanwalberg.com. I also have an email list if you would like to hear from me about new books and other updates. I'm happy to hear input or questions about this book, any of my other books, or whatever other healthcare compliance matters that may be on your mind. Last, if you found this book helpful, please leave a review on Amazon and tell your colleagues. Thank you and keep up the good work!

Acknowledgments

This book was a real challenge owing to the complexity of the subject matter and the continuous changes in both regulations and enforcement. I'm grateful to the subject matter experts and stakeholders who provided suggestions and input, both on the front end and throughout the process. My colleagues at Coordinista, who were all so supportive: Cindy Bauer, Mike McGuire, Nick Welham, took time away from their heavy workloads to review the book and give feedback; Dr. Sam Basta, with whom I had some great discussions and who also took his valuable time to review the book; Pete Celerno, who taught me about the real-life complexities of starting a telehealth practice; and other colleagues: Gail Morrison and Jeff Ellington—thank you for your time with discussion and reviewing the book. All of these people have tremendous insight and experience in the healthcare technology space, and I'm grateful that they were willing to share their knowledge.

In terms of getting this book actually put together and out in the world, I have to first thank Christina Palaia, as always, for great editing but also, in this instance, helping me organize a lot of messy material into something that makes sense! And last but not least, Glen Edelstein, who gave me a beautiful cover, interior design, and a range of input and guidance based on his extensive background. I feel blessed to have such talented people in my universe.

And, also as always, I'm grateful for the friends, family, and colleagues who not only were supportive but also had to hear about exciting things like FTC developments more than they may have wanted. Thanks for being there, and don't worry, I'm sure there will be a Second Edition for you to hear about!

Endnotes

Chapter 1 Healthcare Technology: What Is It?

1 "Getting Started with Telehealth," Telehealth.HHS.gov, Health Resources & Services Administration, https://telehealth.hhs.gov/providers/getting-started#types-of-telehealth.

2 "FTC Warns Health Apps and Connected Device Companies to Comply with Health Breach Notification Rule," Federal Trade Commission, September 15, 2021, https://www.ftc.gov/news-events/news/press-releases/2021/09/ftc-warns-health-apps-connected-device-companies-comply-health-breach-notification-rule.

3 "FTC Proposes Amendments to Strengthen and Modernize the Health Breach Notification Rule," Federal Trade Commission, May 18, 2023, https://www.ftc.gov/news-events/news/press-releases/2023/05/ftc-proposes-amendments-strengthen-modernize-health-breach-notification-rule.

4 Rohit Chopra and Rebecca Kelly Slaughter, "Joint Statement of Commissioner Rohit Chopra and Commissioner Rebecca Kelly Slaughter Concurring in Part, Dissenting in Part in the Matter of Flo Health, Inc., Commission File No. 1923133," Office of Commissioner Rohit Chopra, Federal Trade Commission, January 13, 2021 https://www.ftc.gov/system/files/documents/public_statements/1586018/20210112_final_joint_rcrks_statement_on_flo.pdf.

5 "FTC Finalizes Order with Flo Health, a Fertility-Tracking App That Shared Sensitive Health Data with Facebook, Google, and Others," Federal Trade Commission, June 22, 2021, https://www.ftc.gov/news-events/news/press-releases/2021/06/ftc-finalizes-order-flo-health-fertility-tracking-app-shared-sensitive-health-data-facebook-google.

6 Laurie Pycroft, "Security of Implantable Medical Devices with Wireless Connections: The Dangers of Cyber-Attacks," *Expert Review of Medical Devices* 15, no 6 (2018), https://www.tandfonline.com/doi/full/10.1080/17434440.2018.1483235.

7 Nick Paul Taylor, "DHS Warns of Critical Cybersecurity Weakness with Medtronic Implants," MedTechDive, March 22, 2019, https://www.medtechdive.com/news/dhs-warns-of-critical-cybersecurity-weakness-with-medtronic-implants/551091/.

8 Jill McKeon, "61M Fitbit, Apple Users Had Data Exposed in Wearable Device Data Breach," HealthITSecurity, September 16, 2021, https://healthitsecurity.com/news/61m-fitbit-apple-users-had-data-exposed-in-wearable-device-data-breach.

9 Todd Feathers, Katie Palmer, and Simon Fondrie-Teitler, "'Out of Control': Dozens of Telehealth Startups Sent Sensitive Health Information to Big Tech Companies," *The Markup*, December 13, 2022, https://themarkup.org/pixel-hunt/2022/12/13/out-of-control-dozens-of-telehealth-startups-sent-sensitive-health-information-to-big-tech-companies.

10 Kristin Cohen, "Location, Health, and Other Sensitive Information: FTC Committed to Fully Enforcing the Law Against Illegal Use and Sharing of Highly Sensitive Data," *Business Blog*, Federal Trade Commission, July 11, 2022, https://www.ftc.gov/business-guidance/blog/2022/07/location-health-and-other-sensitive-information-ftc-committed-fully-enforcing-law-against-illegal.

11 "Synchronous Direct-to-Consumer Telehealth," Telehealth.HHS.

com, Health Resources & Services Administration, https://tele-health.hhs.gov/providers/best-practice-guides/direct-to-consumer/synchronous-direct-to-consumer-telehealth.

12 "Asynchronous Direct-to-Consumer Telehealth," Telehealth.HHS.com, Health Resources & Services Administration, https://tele-health.hhs.gov/providers/best-practice-guides/direct-to-consumer/asynchronous-direct-to-consumer-telehealth.

13 "Monthly Telehealth Regional Tracker," FairHealth, https://www.fairhealth.org/fh-trackers/telehealth.

14 "Artificial Intelligence and Machine Learning in Software as a Medical Device," US Food and Drug Administration, last updated September 22, 2021, https://www.fda.gov/medical-devices/software-medical-device-samd/artificial-intelligence-and-machine-learning-software-medical-device.

15 *Proposed Regulatory Framework for Modifications to Artificial Intelligence/Machine Learning (AI/ML)-Based Software as a Medical Device (SaMD)—Discussion Paper and Request for Feedback* (Washington, DC: US Food and Drug Administration, 2019), https://www.fda.gov/files/medical%20devices/published/US-FDA-Artificial-Intelligence-and-Machine-Learning-Discussion-Paper.pdf.

16 Executive Order No. 14110, 88 Fed. Reg. 75191 (October 30, 2023), https://www.federalregister.gov/documents/2023/11/01/2023-24283/safe-secure-and-trustworthy-development-and-use-of-artificial-intelligence.

17 US Patent and Trademark Office, Department of Commerce, "Guidance on Use of Artificial Intelligence-Based Tools in Practice Before the United States Patent and Trademark Office," 89 Fed. Reg. 25609-25617, April 11, 2024, https://www.federalregister.gov/documents/2024/04/11/2024-07629/guidance-on-use-of-artificial-intelligence-based-tools-in-practice-before-the-united-states-patent#citation-2-p25609.

18 "AI-Related Sources," US Patent and Trademark Office, https://www. uspto.gov/initiatives/artificial-intelligence/artificial-intelligence-re-sources?utm_content=&utm_name=&utm_term=.

19 *Proposal for a Regulation of the European Parliament and of the Council Laying Down Harmonised Rules on Artificial Intelligence (Artificial Intelligence Act) and Amending Certain Union Legislative Acts*, Document 52021PC0206 (Brussels: European Commission, April 2021), https://eur-lex.europa. eu/legal-content/EN/TXT/?uri=celex%3A52021PC0206.

20 Spencer Feingold, "The European Union's Artificial Intelligence Act, Explained," World Economic Forum, March 28, 2023, https://www. weforum.org/agenda/2023/03/the-european-union-s-ai-act-explained/.

Chapter 2 Health and Human Services

21 Health Insurance Portability and Accountability Act of 1996, Pub. L. No. 104-191, 110 Stat. 1936 (1996). All definitions in this section come from this law.

22 The HITECH Act was enacted as Title XIII of Division A and Title IV of Division B of the American Recovery and Reinvestment Act of 2009 (ARRA), Pub. L. No. 111-5, 123 Stat. 115-521 (2009).

23 "Optum Medical Care," resolution agreement, US Department of Health and Human Services, November 15, 2023, https://www.hhs.gov/hipaa/ for-professionals/compliance-enforcement/agreements/optum-medi-cal-care.html.

24 45 C.F.R. § 153.502.

25 See "HIPAA FAQs for Professionals" at https://www.hhs.gov/hipaa/ for-professionals/faq/index.html.

26 45 C.F.R. §§ 164.308–164.312.

27 "HHS' Office for Civil Rights Settles First Ever Phishing Cyber-Attack

Investigation," press release, US Department of Health and Human Services, December 7, 2023, https://www.hhs.gov/about/news/2023/12/07/hhs-office-for-civil-rights-settles-first-ever-phishing-cyber-attack-investigation.html.

28 "Breach Notification Rule," US Department of Health and Human Services, last reviewed July 26, 2013, https://www.hhs.gov/hipaa/for-professionals/breach-notification/index.html.

Chapter 3 Health and Human Services: Office of the National Coordinator for Health Information Technology and Others

29 "Health IT Legislation," Office of the National Coordinator for Health Information Technology, https://www.healthit.gov/topic/laws-regulation-and-policy/health-it-legislation.

30 US Department of Health and Human Services, "21st Century Cures Act: Interoperability, Information Blocking, and the ONC Health IT Certification Program," 85 Fed. Reg. 25642–25961 (May 1, 2020).

31 "The ONC Cures Act Final Rule," Office of the National Coordinator for Health Information Technology, https://www.healthit.gov/sites/default/files/page2/2020-03/TheONCCuresActFinalRule.pdf.

32 "Information Blocking," Office of the National Coordinator for Health Information Technology, last reviewed April 15, 2024, https://www.healthit.gov/topic/information-blocking.

33 E. Hatef, M. Austin, S. H. Scholle, and B. Buckley, *Evidence- and Consensus-Based Digital Healthcare Equity Framework,* AHRQ Publication No. 24-0020-1-EF (Rockville, MD: Agency for Healthcare Research and Quality, February 2024), https://digital.ahrq.gov/sites/default/files/docs/citation/health-equity-framework.pdf.

34 Pat G. Ouellette and Lara D. Compton, "Biden Executive Order Calls for HHS to Establish HealthCare-Specific

Artificial Intelligence Programs and Policies," *National Law Review*, November 2, 2023, https://natlawreview.com/article/biden-executive-order-calls-hhs-establish-health-care-specific-artificial.

Chapter 4 Food and Drug Administration

35 "Artificial Intelligence and Machine Learning (AI/ML)-Enabled Medical Devices," US Food and Drug Administration, updated May 13, 2024, https://www.fda.gov/medical-devices/software-medical-device-samd/artificial-intelligence-and-machine-learning-aiml-enabled-medical-devices.

36 "Artificial Intelligence and Machine Learning in Software as a Medical Device," US Food And Drug Administration, https://www.fda.gov/medical-devices/software-medical-device-samd/artificial-intelligence-and-machine-learning-software-medical-device. See also: "Premarket Notification 510(k)," US Food and Drug Administration, https://www.fda.gov/medical-devices/premarket-submissions-selecting-and-preparing-correct-submission/premarket-notification-510k; "De Novo Classification Request," US Food and Drug Administration, https://www.fda.gov/medical-devices/premarket-submissions-selecting-and-preparing-correct-submission/de-novo-classification-request; "Premarket Approval (PMA)," US Food and Drug Administration, https://www.fda.gov/medical-devices/premarket-submissions-selecting-and-preparing-correct-submission/premarket-approval-pma; *Proposed Regulatory Framework for Modifications to Artificial Intelligence/Machine Learning (AI/ML)-Based Software as a Medical Device (SaMD)—Discussion Paper and Request for Feedback* (Silver Spring, MD: FDA, 2019), https://www.fda.gov/media/122535/download; "International Medical Device Regulators Forum (IMDRF)," US Food And Drug Administration, https://www.fda.gov/medical-devices/cdrh-international-programs/international-medical-device-regulators-forum-imdrf; Center for Devices and Radiological Health, "Deciding When to Submit a 510(k) for a Change to an Existing Device," US Food and Drug Administration, October 2017, https://

www.fda.gov/regulatory-information/search-fda-guidance-documents/deciding-when-submit-510k-change-existing-device; and *Developing Software Precertification Program: A Working Model* (Silver Spring, MD: FDA, June 2018), https://www.fda.gov/media/113802/download.

37 See Title 21, Chapter I, Subchapter H, Part 801—Labeling, https://www.ecfr.gov/current/title-21/chapter-I/subchapter-H/part-801.

38 International Medical Device Regulators Forum (IMDRF): https://www.imdrf.org/.

39 Center for Devices and Radiological Health, *Best Practices for Communicating Cybersecurity Vulnerabilities to Patients* (Silver Spring, MD: FDA, October 2021), https://www.fda.gov/media/152608/download.

40 Center for Devices and Radiological Health, *Best Practices for Communicating Cybersecurity Vulnerabilities*, https://www.fda.gov/media/152608/download.

41 "About the Digital Health Center of Excellence," US Food and Drug Administration, September 22, 2020, https://www.fda.gov/medical-devices/digital-health-center-excellence/about-digital-health-center-excellence.

Chapter 5 Federal Trade Commission

42 "Privacy and Security," Federal Trade Commission, https://www.ftc.gov/business-guidance/privacy-security.

43 "A Brief Overview of the Federal Trade Commission's Investigative, Law Enforcement, and Rulemaking Authority," Federal Trade Commission, revised May 2021, https://www.ftc.gov/about-ftc/mission/enforcement-authority.

44 "FTC Enforcement Action to Bar GoodRx from Sharing Consumers' Sensitive Health Info for Advertising," press release, Federal Trade Commission, February 1, 2023, https://www.ftc.gov/news-events/news/press-releases/2023/02ftc-enforcement-action-bar-goodrx-shar-

ing-consumers-sensitive-health-info-advertising.

45 15 USC §§ 41–58, as amended.

46 "FTC Gives Final Approval to Settlement with Emergency Travel Services Provider Related to Allegations It Failed to Secure Sensitive Data," press release, Federal Trade Commission, February 5, 2021, https://www.ftc.gov/news-events/news/press-releases/2021/02/ftc-gives-final-approval-settlement-emergency-travel-services-provider-related-allegations-it-failed.

47 "FTC Issues Opinion Finding that TurboTax Maker Intuit Inc. Engaged in Deceptive Practices," press release, Federal Trade Commission, January 22, 2024, https://www.ftc.gov/news-events/news/press-releases/2024/01/ftc-issues-opinion-finding-turbotax-maker-intuit-inc-engaged-deceptive-practices.

48 *Protecting Children's Privacy Under COPPA: A Survey on Compliance*, staff report (Federal Trade Commission, April 2022), https://www.ftc.gov/sites/default/files/documents/reports/protecting-childrens-privacy-under-coppa-survey-compliance/coppasurvey.pdf.

Chapter 6 Fraud and Abuse

49 "The False Claims Act: A Primer," US Department of Justice, https://www.justice.gov/sites/default/files/civil/legacy/2011/04/22/C-FRAUDS_FCA_Primer.pdf.

50 "Jelly Bean Communications Design and Its Manager Settle False Claims Act Liability for Cybersecurity Failures on Florida Medicaid Enrollment Website," press release, Office of Public Affairs, US Department of Justice, March 14, 2023, https://www.justice.gov/opa/pr/jelly-bean-communications-design-and-its-manager-settle-false-claims-act-liability.

51 United States of America, ex rel. Patricia Crocano, v. Trividia Health Inc., Case No. 22-CV-60160-RAR (S.D. Fla. 2022), https://www.

gibsondunn.com/wp-content/uploads/2023/10/US-Statement-of-Interest-in-U.S.-ex-rel-Crocono-v-Trividia-Health.pdf.

52 42 U.S.C. 1320a-7(h).

53 "Modernizing Medicine Agrees to Pay $45 Million to Resolve Allegations of Accepting and Paying Illegal Kickbacks and Causing False Claims," press release, Office of Public Affairs, US Department of Justice, November 1, 2022, https://www.justice.gov/opa/pr/modernizing-medicine-agrees-pay-45-million-resolve-allegations-accepting-and-paying-illegal.

Chapter 7 Industry Compliance Guidance

54 "Electronic Health Records Technology Vendor to Pay $18.25 Million to Resolve Kickback Allegations," press release, Office of Public Affairs, US Department of Justice, January 28, 2021, https://www.justice.gov/opa/pr/electronic-health-records-technology-vendor-pay-1825-million-resolve-kickback-allegations.

55 See "AdvaMed Code of Ethics," AdvaMed, June 1, 2023, https://www.advamed.org/member-center/resource-library/advamed-code-of-ethics/.

Chapter 9 Telehealth and Virtual Care: Setup and Operations

56 Multistate licensure compacts streamline the licensing process across states through one application, while preserving state oversight of quality.

57 "Participating States," Interstate Medical Licensure Compact, https://www.imlcc.org/participating-states/.

58 "General FAQs About the Compact," Interstate Medical Licensure Compact, https://www.imlcc.org/faqs/.

59 "Licensure Compacts," Telehealth.HHS.gov, last updated April 20, 2023, https://telehealth.hhs.gov/licensure/licensure-compacts.

60 FSMB Workgroup on Telemedicine, *The Appropriate Use of Telemedicine Technologies in the Practice of Medicine* (Washington, DC: Federation of State Medical Boards, 2022), https://www.fsmb.org/siteassets/advocacy/policies/fsmb-workgroup-on-telemedicineapril-2022-final.pdf.

61 "The Joint Commission Launches Telehealth Accreditation," The Joint Commission, April 23, 2024, https://www.jointcommission.org/resources/news-and-multimedia/news/2024/04/the-joint-commission-launches-telehealth-accreditation/.

62 Office for Civil Rights (OCR), "Guidance on How the HIPAA Rules Permit Covered Health Care Providers and Health Plans to Use Remote Communication Technologies for Audio-Only Telehealth," US Department of Health and Human Services, last reviewed June 13, 2022, https://www.hhs.gov/hipaa/for-professionals/privacy/guidance/hipaa-audio-telehealth/index.html.

63 *50-State Survey: Establishment of a Patient-Physician Relationship via Telemedicine* (Chicago: American Medical Association, 2018), https://www.ama-assn.org/system/files/2018-10/ama-chart-telemedicine-patient-physician-relationship.pdf.

64 See "Federally Qualified Health Centers (FQHC) Center," CMS.gov, last modified September 21, 2023, https://www.cms.gov/center/provider-type/federally-qualified-health-centers-fqhc-center.

65 "Physician Fee Schedule," CMS.gov, last updated November 2, 2022, https://www.cms.gov/medicare/medicare-fee-for-service-payment/physicianfeesched.

66 "Telehealth Policy Changes After the COVID-19 Public Health Emergency," Telehealth.HHS.gov, last updated June 7, 2023, https://telehealth.hhs.gov/providers/policy-changes-during-the-covid-19-public-health-emergency/policy-changes-after-the-covid-19-public-health-emergency#permanent-medicare-changes.

67 Pub. L. No. 110-425, 122 Stat. 4820 (2008).

68 21 U.S.C. Section 829(e)(3).

69 Substance Abuse and Mental Health Services Administration, Department of Health and Human Services, "Medications for the Treatment of Opioid Use Disorder," 89 Fed. Reg. 7528 (February 2, 2024), https://www.federalregister.gov/documents/2024/02/02/2024-01693/medications-for-the-treatment-of-opioid-use-disorder. The PDF for public review is at https://public-inspection.federalregister.gov/2024-01693.pdf.

70 "Telehealth," Office of Inspector General, US Department of Health and Human Services, last updated June 16, 2023, https://oig.hhs.gov/reports-and-publications/featured-topics/telehealth/.

Chapter 10 Occupational Safety and Health Administration

71 See "Help for Employers," Occupational Safety and Health Administration, https://www.osha.gov/employers.

72 *Recommended Practices for Anti-Retaliation Programs* (Washington, DC: Occupational Safety and Health Administration, n.d.), https://www.osha.gov/sites/default/files/publications/OSHA3905.pdf.

73 "Harassment," US Equal Employment Opportunity Commission, https://www.eeoc.gov/harassment.

74 "Search the Exclusions Database," Office of Inspector General, US Department of Health and Human Services, https://exclusions.oig.hhs.gov.

75 "Federal Contractors and Grantees," Substance Abuse and Mental Health Services Administration, https://www.samhsa.gov/workplace/employer-resources/contractor-grantee-laws; and "Chapter 10—Drug-Free Workplace," 41 U.S.C. § 701. (2009), https://www.govinfo.gov/content/pkg/USCODE-2009-title41/pdf/USCODE-2009-title41-chap10.pdf.

76 *Stone et al. v. Salem Community Hospital et al.* (N.D. Ohio 2023), https://www.documentcloud.org/documents/24235588-salem_data_breach_suit; and Steve Alder, "Concentra Confirms Almost 4 Million Patients Affected by PJ&A Data Breach," HIPAA Journal, January 31, 2024, https://www.hipaajournal.com/pja-data-breach/.

www.ingramcontent.com/pod-product-compliance
Lightning Source LLC
Chambersburg PA
CBHW031850200326
41597CB00012B/349